Word® 6 for Windows™ Essentials

Linda Hefferin
Elgin Community College
&
Laura Acklen

QUE
COLLEGE

Word 6 for Windows Essentials

Library of Congress Catalog No.: 94-69260

ISBN: 0-7897-0108-1

98 97 96 95   4 3

Interpretation of the printing code: the rightmost double-digit number is the year of the book's printing; the rightmost single-digit number, the number of the book's printing. For example, a printing code of 95-1 shows that the first printing of the book occurred in 1995.

Screens reproduced in this book were created using Collage Plus from Inner Media, Inc., Hollis, NH.

Word 6 for Windows Essentials is based on Word 6 for Windows.

Publisher: David P. Ewing

Associate Publisher: Paul Boger

Publishing Manager: Chris Katsaropoulos

Marketing Manager: Susan Dollman

Managing Editor: Sheila Cunningham

Production Editor: Beth Hux

Cover Designer: Dan Armstrong

Cover Illustration: Michael McGurl

Book Designer: Paula A. Carroll

Acquisitions Coordinator: Elizabeth D. Brown

Production Team: Claudia Bell, Amy Cornwell, Anne Dickerson, Karen Gregor, Aren Howell, Daryl Kessler, Beth Lewis, Mike Thomas, Stephen Carlin, Steph Mineart

About the Authors

Linda Hefferin is a full-time professor in the Business Division at Elgin Community College in Elgin, Illinois. In addition to teaching WordPerfect and Microsoft Word, she teaches a variety of other types of applications including spreadsheet, graphics, database, and personal information management. Linda is a Certified Novell ® Instructor and author or co-author of several Que books.

Dedicated to TMD.

Laura Acklen is an independent author and instructor located in Austin, Texas. She has been training and supporting computer users in DOS and Windows products since 1986. Laura has written over 15 student manuals and instructor guides for the national training company, Productivity Point International. She is the author of Que's *WordPerfect 6.0 SureSteps* and co-author of *Oops! WordPerfect...What To Do When Things Go Wrong*. She is also a contributing author of *Using WordPerfect Version 6 for Windows*, Special Edition, *Using WordPerfect Version 6.1 for Windows*, Special Edition and the revision author for *Windows QuickStart*, 3.11 Edition. Her most recent project is Que's *First Look at Windows 95*.

To Chris and Beth, for all your good humor and enthusiastic support.

Acknowledgments

Que College is grateful for the assistance provided by the following reviewers: Colleen Ceraolo, Broward Community College—Central Campus. And thank you to our technical editor, Michelle Poolet.

Trademark Acknowledgments

All terms mentioned in this book that are known to be trademarks or service marks have been appropriately capitalized. Que cannot attest to the accuracy of this information. Use of a term in this book should not be regarded as affecting the validity of any trademark or service mark.

Word 6 is a trademark of and Microsoft, Microsoft Windows, and MS-DOS are registered trademarks of Microsoft Corporation.

IBM is a registered trademark of International Business Machines Corporation.

Preface

Que College is the educational publishing imprint of Macmillan Computer Publshing, the world's leading computer book publisher. Macmillan Computer Publishing books have taught over 20 million people how to be productive with their computer.

This expertise in producing high-quality computer tutorial and reference books is also evident in every Que College title we publish. The same tried and true authoring and product development process that makes Macmillan Computer Publishing books bestsellers is used to ensure that every Que College textbook has the most accurate and most up-to-date information. Experienced and respected college instructors write and review every manuscript to provide class-tested pedagogy. Quality assurance editors check every keystroke and command in Que College books to ensure that instructions are clear and precise.

Above all, Macmillan Computer Publishing and, in turn, Que College, has years of experience at meeting the learning demands of computer users in business and at home. This "real-world" experience means Que College textbooks help students understand how the skills they learn will be applied and why these skills are important.

The "Essentials" of Hands-On Learning

Thank you for using the ***Essentials*** series in your classroom. This collection of hands-on tutorials is designed to be used separately or as computer lab application modules to accompany *Computers in Your Future* by Marilyn Meyer and Roberta Baber of Fresno City College. The four-color modules, presented in a project-driven chapter format, cover the fundamental elements of each application. The tutorials are designed for a broad spectrum of majors, although the business case problems contained in the end-of-chapter material also make them suitable for use in Schools of Business. Each ***Essentials*** volume is four-color throughout, and sized at 8 1/2" x 11" for maximum screen shot visibility.

Project Objectives list what your student will do and learn from each project.

Why Would I Do This? shows your student why this material is essential.

Step-by-Step Tutorials simplify the procedure with large screen shots, captions, and annotations.

If you have problems... anticipates common pitfalls and advises your student accordingly.

Inside Stuff provides tips and shortcuts for more effective applications.

Key Terms are highlighted in the text and defined in the margin when they first appear.

Jargon Watch offers a layman's view of "technobabble" in easily understandable terms.

Concepts Sidebars showcase intriguing topics normally covered in the Concepts course, and serve to integrate pertinent material with Meyer/Baber's *Computers in Your Future*.

Checking Your Skills provides True/False, Multiple Choice, Completion, and Screen Labeling exercises.

Applying Your Skills contains hands-on case studies that test students' critical thinking skills and ability to apply what they've learned. The *On Your Own* case study lets students use their newly learned skills in a personally-oriented application. *Brief Cases* test the student's skills in a business environment

The Essentials series covers the following applications in both Windows 3.1 and Windows 95 versions:

1-2-3 Release 5 for Windows

Excel 5 for Windows

Access 2 for Windows

Microsoft Office

Works 3 for Windows

WordPerfect 6 for Windows

Paradox 5 for Windows

Quattro Pro 6 for Windows

The series also includes manuals on Internet, Windows 3.1, and Windows 95.

An Instructor's Manual contains suggested curriculum guides for courses of varying lengths, teaching tips, answers to questions appearing in the **Checking Your Skills** and **Applying Your Skills** sections, test questions (and answers), additional projects, and a data disk with files for the text's step-by-step tutorials. The Instructor's Manual is available by request to teachers upon adoption of any of the **Essentials** manuals. Please contact your local representative or write to us on school letterhead at Macmillan Computer Publishing, 201 W. 103rd Street, Indianapolis, IN 46290-1097, Attn: S. Dollman.

The Que College commitment to the educational market demands that we listen and respond to the needs of professors and students. At Que College, our most important partners are you, the end users. To help us continue to provide you with the best in computer education, we look to you for continual feedback. If you have any questions or comments regarding this product, or are interested in acting as a reviewer on future endeavors, please write to Chris Katsaropoulos, Publishing Manager, Macmillan Computer Publishing, 201 W. 103rd Street, Indianapolis, IN 46290-1097.

Que College
Publishing for tomorrow...*today.*

Table of Contents at a Glance

Table of Contents

Project 1

Getting Started with Word for Windows

In this project, you learn how to

- Start Word for Windows
- Use the Word Screen
- Use Menus and Dialog Boxes
- Customize Word
- Get Help
- Exit Word

Why Would I Do This?

Word processing software is the most common application software used on *personal computers*. It's estimated that some form of word processing software is installed on 95 percent of the personal computers in use. Word processing software is easy to use, and nearly everyone has some reason to use it. As you work through the projects in this book, you will discover why word processing software such as Word for Windows is so popular.

Word for Windows lets you create, modify, and format *documents* quickly and easily. In this project, you begin learning how Word works and what you can do with Word by starting the software and taking a tour of the Word screen. You learn how to customize Word, and you learn how to use the Help system—an invaluable tool when you are just starting to use this program. After becoming familiar with Word, you learn how to exit the program successfully.

Lesson 1: Starting Word

The first thing you need to know about Word for Windows is how to start the software. Because you start Word for Windows from the Windows Program Manager, you must open Windows before you go any further. If you are not familiar with Windows or with using the mouse, see the *Working with Windows* Appendix at the end of this book for help.

Starting Word is simple to do—it's as easy as starting your car. Try starting Word now.

To Start Word

❶ Turn on the computer and monitor.

At this point, most computers display technical information about the computer and the operating software installed on the machine. The computer will probably display the *DOS* prompt (C:\>).

❷ At the DOS prompt (C:\>), type WIN, and then press ↵Enter.

The computer loads Windows, and the Windows *Program Manager* should appear on-screen as shown in Figure 1.1. (Your screen may look slightly different, depending on how Windows is set up on your computer.) The Program Manager indicates that you are in Windows, which means you can now start Word for Windows.

It's possible that when you turn on your machine, Windows may start automatically, or you may be able to start Windows by using a menu set up for your system. Also, if your computer is part of a network of computers, your start-up procedures may be different.

❸ Locate the Word for Windows icon (see Figure 1.1).

The Word *icon* should appear in a *group window* that has a title such as "WFW 6.0." If the window is not open, open the program *group icon* by double-clicking the icon using the mouse. Depending on your setup, the group window/icon may have a different name, such as "Word for Windows."

Figure 1.1
The Windows Program Manager and the Windows Apps group window.

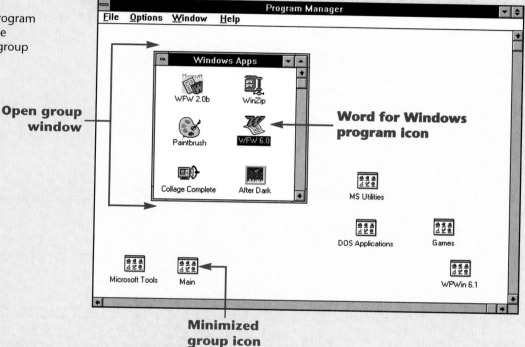

If you have problems

If you can't find the Word for Windows program icon in an open window and you can't locate the program group icon, try opening other minimized program groups to search for the Word program icon. The Word icon may be located in another program group with a title such as Word for Windows, Microsoft Office, or Windows Applications.

❹ Double-click the Word for Windows program icon.

This action starts Word for Windows, and a blank document appears on your screen (see Figure 1.2).

continues

To Start Word (continued)

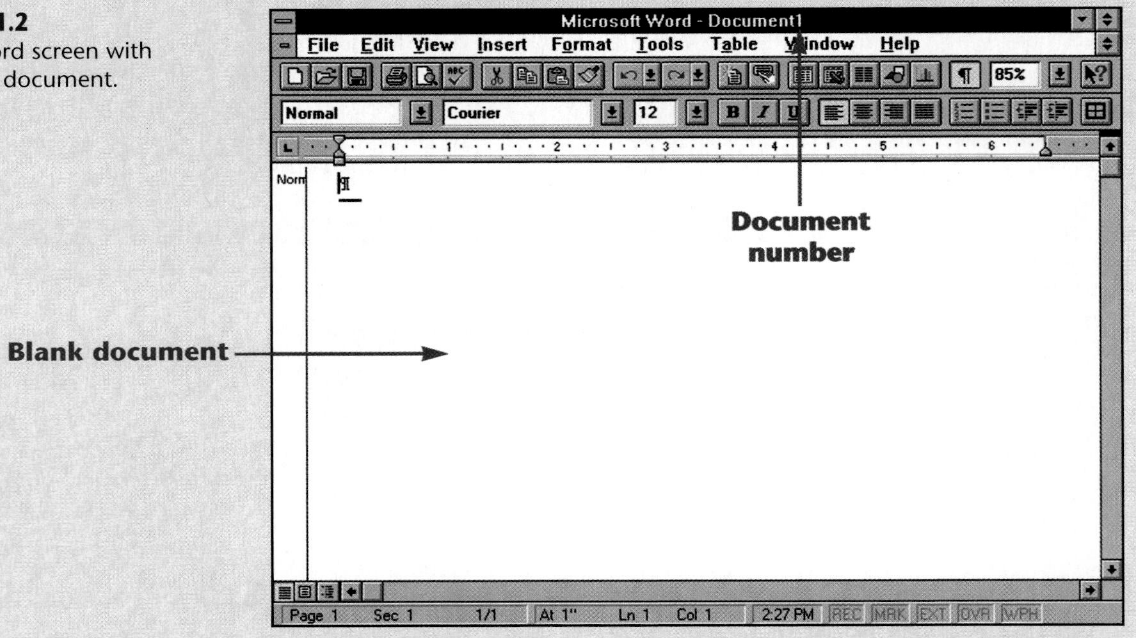

Figure 1.2
The Word screen with
a blank document.

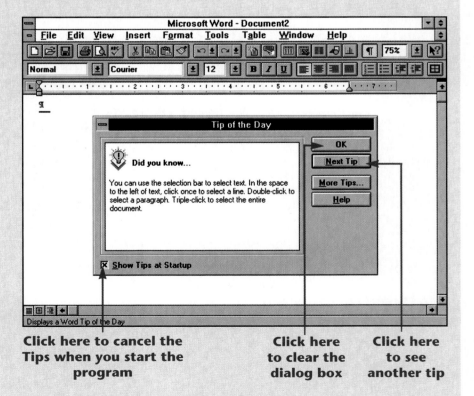

Blank document

**Document
number**

If the Tip of the Day feature is activated, a Tip of the Day dialog box
(see Figure 1.3) appears on-screen. These tips are very helpful when
you are learning the program. After you read the tip, choose OK to
clear the dialog box.

Figure 1.3
The Tip of the Day
dialog box.

**Click here to cancel the
Tips when you start the
program**

**Click here
to clear the
dialog box**

**Click here
to see
another tip**

Jargon Watch

You had to wade through a lot of computer jargon in Lesson 1, probably your first experience using Word. Throughout this book, key terms are defined for you where they are first used, but when a number of these computer terms are introduced in the same lesson, a Jargon Watch box like this one appears to help take some of the mystery out of the words.

The term **DOS** stands for Disk Operating System, which acts as a translator between you and the computer. Typing a word at the DOS prompt simply tells the computer what you want to do. For example, when you typed WIN at the DOS prompt, DOS converted that simple command into machine language commands, which told the computer to start the Windows software.

The Windows **Program Manager** does just what the name implies—it manages your programs. Every program has a **program icon**, or picture. Clicking a program icon opens the program that icon represents. Similar program icons are grouped together in **group windows**. When a group window opens, you can see the program icons inside. When a group window is closed (or minimized), it is represented by a **group icon**. (Refer to Figure 1.1, which shows examples of group windows, group icons, and program icons).

Lesson 2: Using the Word Screen

With Word for Windows up and running on your computer, it's time to tour the Word screen. Many elements of the Word screen may be familiar to you from your work with other Windows programs—elements like the Minimize and Maximize buttons, Control-menus, and scroll bars. Other parts of the screen are features of Word for Windows that can help you complete your work quickly and efficiently. For example, the toolbars and Ruler are convenient tools that you use in most of the projects in this book.

Because Word is a Windows application, it operates under the same rules as other Windows programs. For example, each application opens into a *window*, much like the Program Manager window. One difference, however, is that most applications have separate controls for the application window and the document window. Figure 1.4 shows the *Control-menu* and *Minimize/Maximize buttons* on the *title bar* as well as those on the *menu bar*. The controls on the title bar are for the application window; the controls on the menu bar are for the document window. Again, for more information on common parts of the Windows screen, see the *Working with Windows* Appendix at the end of this book.

When you see only File & Help - type ALT V for rules & tool bars or windows at top

Tool bars - float - to set it at top - click standard OK.

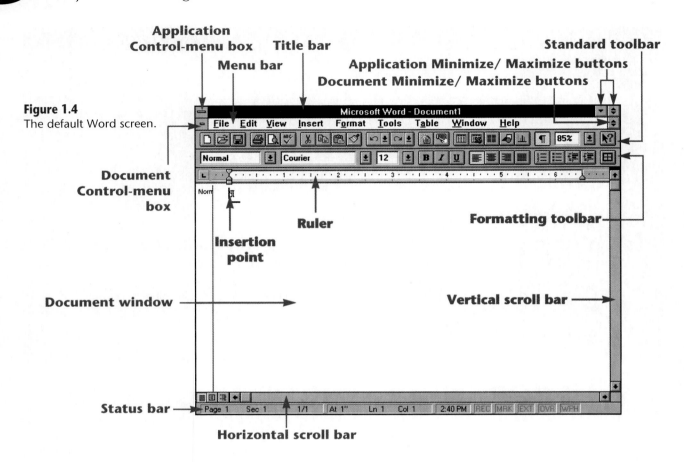

Figure 1.4
The default Word screen.

The following table lists the default Word for Windows 6.0 screen elements and gives a brief description of each element.

Table 1.1   Word Screen Elements

Element	Description
Title bar	Used to show the current document number or the name, if the document has been named. Unnamed documents are temporarily named by Word with sequential numbers (1,2,3).
Menu bar	Lists the available main menus and gives you access to the pull-down menu system. You can use both the mouse and the keyboard to access pull-down menus.
Toolbar	A strip of icons that you click with the mouse to access frequently used features. Each icon contains a picture that illustrates the feature.

Element	Description
Ruler	Accessible only with a mouse, the Ruler adjusts tabs, indents, left/right margins, and table columns.
Insertion point	Indicates your location on-screen; also indicates where text you type will be inserted in the document window.
Document window	Area where you type, edit, and format your document.
Vertical scroll bar	Accessible only with a mouse, the vertical scroll bar is used to move up and down in a document.
Horizontal scroll bar	Accessible only with a mouse, the horizontal scroll bar is used to move from left to right in a document.
Status bar	Displays the current page number, the position of the insertion point on the page, the time, and whether or not certain features are in use. When selecting a menu item, a brief description of the currently selected item is displayed.
Application Control-menu box	Displays the application's Control-menu. Double-click the application Control-menu box to exit (or close) the application.
Application Minimize/Maximize buttons	Used to minimize, maximize, and restore the application window.
Document Control-menu box	Displays the document's Control-menu. Double-click the document Control-menu box to close the document.
Document Minimize/Maximize buttons	Used to minimize, maximize, and restore the document window.

Refer to Table 1.1 for descriptions of the different screen elements. See Figure 1.4 to help you find your way around the screen. Now try getting to know the elements of the Word for Windows screen.

To Use the Word Screen

❶ Using the mouse, click File to open the File menu.

Notice that Word's menus look similar to the menus in any Windows program. In Word, you can open menus and choose commands to perform actions. You can cancel a menu by clicking the menu name again, clicking anywhere in the document window outside of the menu, or by pressing Esc.

❷ To cancel or close the File menu, click File again using the mouse.

❸ Move the mouse pointer to the title bar.

The title bar contains the name of the program and the name of the current document, as well as other Window elements such as the Maximize and Minimize buttons (refer to Figure 1.4).

❹ Move the mouse pointer to the Print icon on the Standard Toolbar.

The second and third lines of the Word for Windows screen are toolbars, which contain a series of *icons* (refer to Figure 1.4). These icons represent commonly used menu commands. For example, clicking the **P**rint icon is the same as choosing **F**ile, **P**rint.

Notice that when you point to an element on one of the toolbars, Word displays a brief description of that element. These descriptions, called ToolTips, come in handy when you can't remember what a particular icon does.

❺ Move the mouse pointer to the second drop-down list arrow on the Formatting toolbar.

This is the Font drop-down list, which indicates the currently selected font (refer to Figure 1.4). Clicking the drop-down arrow next to the Font drop-down list lets you scroll through the list of available fonts.

❻ Move the mouse pointer into the document window.

Notice how the mouse pointer changes from a left-facing arrow to an object that looks like the letter "I." This is called an I-beam. Anytime the mouse pointer appears within the document window, it displays as an I-beam.

Jargon Watch

Icons are small pictures that represent common actions you can perform—generally, the most common actions you perform in a word processing program. Clicking an icon with the left mouse button selects the action represented by the icon. For example, clicking the **O**pen icon (open file folder) lets you open an existing file.

Lesson 3: Using Menus and Dialog Boxes

Word's menu bar, located directly below the title bar, contains menu names; you open these menus to list Word commands. You use these commands to do things in Word, such as editing or formatting text.

In Word, choosing commands with an ellipsis next to them opens a dialog box. Dialog boxes present a number of options and ask you to choose what you want to do. Try using menus and dialog boxes in Word now.

To Use Menus and Dialog Boxes

❶ Move the mouse pointer to Format on the menu bar, and click the left mouse button.

The Format menu lists all the commands you can use to format your documents. Once a menu opens, you can click a command with the mouse to select the command.

❷ Drag the mouse down the list to highlight the various menu commands; then choose Paragraph.

Word displays the Paragraph dialog box (see Figure 1.5).

Figure 1.5
The Paragraph dialog box shows the commands used to format text in a paragraph.

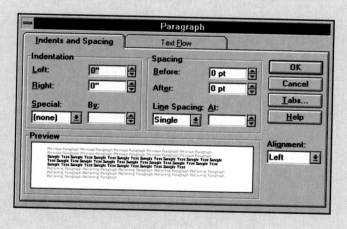

❸ Click the Cancel button.

You use the Cancel button when you want to close a dialog box without making any changes.

❹ Choose File from the menu bar.

The File menu appears. Once a menu opens, you can select a command with the keyboard by using the up and down arrow keys to move through the available menu items.

The ellipsis (...) next to the Open command tells you that a dialog box appears to provide you with further options after you select Open.

continues

To Use Menus and Dialog Boxes (continued)

❺ **Press the ⬇ one time; then press ↵Enter.**

This action chooses the **O**pen command. The Open dialog box appears as shown in Figure 1.6.

Figure 1.6
The Open dialog box is used to open files you have already saved to a disk.

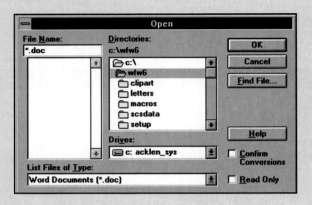

❻ **Click the Cancel button.**

Clicking the Cancel button closes the dialog box without selecting any options or performing any actions. In the next lesson, you learn how to customize Word.

If you prefer to use the keyboard to open the menus, you can press ⟨Alt⟩ plus the underlined letter. For example, to open the **F**ile menu, you press ⟨Alt⟩+⟨F⟩. Once the menu opens, however, you just press the underlined letter (without the ⟨Alt⟩ key).

Word uses symbols in its menus to let you know what happens when you select a menu item. Many commands need more information from you before the computer can carry out the command. You give this information either by responding to dialog boxes, or by choosing a more specific command.

If you see an ellipsis (...) next to an item, that means a dialog box appears when you select that item. A check mark next to a menu item means that item is already selected (or turned on). If you don't see anything next to an item (**Ex**it on the **F**ile menu, for example), that command doesn't need any more information from you.

Shortcut keys appear next to some menu items. These keys give you fast ways to choose Word commands without leaving the keyboard. For example, the shortcut key for the **O**pen command on the **F**ile menu is ⟨Ctrl⟩+⟨O⟩. Once you learn shortcut keys, you can use these keys to open the menus.

The Short, Happy Life of the Wang

What does the word Wang mean to you? During the late 70s and early 80s, the term *Wang* became synonymous with word processing. At that time, Wang word processing systems were the undisputed leaders in the word processing market, and although its success was short-lived, Wang contributed many of the features used in word processing software today.

Wang was founded by Dr. An Wang, a brilliant Chinese immigrant who built a corporate giant from scratch. Wang introduced the first CRT-based word processing system in 1976, and within two years of its development, Wang became the largest worldwide supplier of such systems. Wang word processing systems consisted of a central processing unit that served several terminals dedicated only to the task of word processing the Wang way.

During the 1970s, Wang Labs grew at an annual rate of 67 percent. The value of Wang stock skyrocketed from $6 per share in 1976 to $800 per share in 1983! By 1985, Wang had developed into a worldwide giant with over 30,000 employees

year. In only four years, the company's stock had lost more than 90 percent of its value, during the greatest boom market in history.

What happened to Wang? Even during Wang's heyday, warning signs indicated trouble ahead. The company had borrowed and expanded with unrestrained optimism. The twelve-story corporate headquarters had lavish decorations, and top management traveled in a $14 million corporate jet that even included china bearing the Wang logo.

The days of dedicated word processing were numbered by 1981, when IBM introduced its Personal Computer. At first, word processing software for microcomputers didn't have all the features available on the Wang. Soon, however, products such as WordPerfect, WordStar, and Multimate boasted of powerful word processing capabilities.

At first, Wang's customers were slow to abandon their sizable investment in Wang equipment. Law firms stayed especially loyal to Wang because many of the lawyers didn't want to have computers on their desks. Yet, companies soon realized that PCs offered more power and flexibility than a machine like the Wang, which was dedicated to one specific task.

Wang was a multibillion-dollar company, but it was slow to adapt to the new PC world. The personal computer rapidly replaced the Wang, as the company watched its market leadership slip away. Nonetheless, Wang word processing will always be remembered for its contribution to PC software, such as Word and WordPerfect, that is used today.

and revenues of $3 billion. The people of Wang began to think anything was possible under the guidance of their enigmatic founder, universally known as the Doctor. By 1989, however, Wang sustained a stunning $424 million loss for the fiscal

For further information relating to this topic, see Unit 4A, "Word Processing and Desktop Publishing," of **Computers in Your Future** *by Marilyn Meyer and Roberta Baber.*

Lesson 4: Customizing Word

Default
Automatic settings that the computer uses unless you specify other settings.

As you have seen, the *default* Word screen contains two toolbars and a Ruler to help you quickly accomplish common tasks. If you prefer, you can turn these elements off so that they don't display on-screen, which gives you more room on your screen for text. You can also make changes to the keyboard, the toolbars, and the menus to suit your preferences. In Word, you make these changes from the Customize dialog box.

You can also customize many areas of the program to suit your unique work habits by using the Options dialog box. When you modify these settings, the changes take effect immediately and remain in effect until you change them again.

In this lesson, you learn how to turn the display of the toolbars and the Ruler on and off, as well as how to use the **C**ustomize and **O**ptions tools.

To Customize Word

❶ Choose View from the menu bar.

The **V**iew menu has options for the toolbars and the Ruler (see Figure 1.7). A check mark appears next to a menu command when that screen element is turned on. Notice the check mark next to the Ruler, which is turned on by default.

Figure 1.7
The **V**iew menu commands let you customize the Word screen.

Check mark ⟶

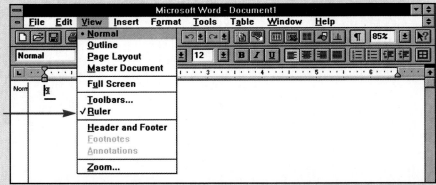

❷ Choose Ruler from the View menu.

Because the Ruler is turned on by default, when you choose **R**uler, your action "deselects" the option and turns the Ruler off. Look at the top of the screen, and notice that you can no longer see the Ruler.

Toggle switch
A single menu command used to turn a feature both on and off. If the feature is already on, selecting the menu command turns it off, and vice versa.

❸ From the menu bar, choose View.

Now that you have turned the Ruler off, the check mark no longer appears next to the menu command. The command to display the Ruler is a *toggle switch*. If the Ruler is already displayed, selecting the menu command turns the command off; if the Ruler is not displayed, selecting the menu command turns the command on.

④ Choose Ruler.

The Ruler reappears on-screen, below the toolbars. In the next step, you control the display of the toolbars.

⑤ From the menu bar, choose View; then choose Toolbars.

The Toolbars dialog box is displayed (see Figure 1.8); this dialog box lets you choose which toolbars you want displayed. By default, the Standard and Formatting toolbars are selected. These two options have an X in the check box next to them, indicating that they are currently selected. Because you use the default toolbars in later lessons, you need to leave them displayed on-screen.

Figure 1.8
The Toolbars dialog box lets you display or hide toolbars.

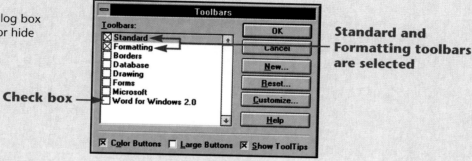

Standard and Formatting toolbars are selected

Check box

⑥ Click the Cancel button.

This action cancels the Toolbars dialog box without making any changes.

⑦ Choose Tools from the menu bar; then choose Customize.

You can use the Customize dialog box to make changes to the toolbars, the menus, and the keyboard (see Figure 1.9). The tabs at the top of the dialog box let you switch to different pages in the dialog box.

Tabs

Figure 1.9
The Customize dialog box lets you modify toolbars, menus, and the keyboard.

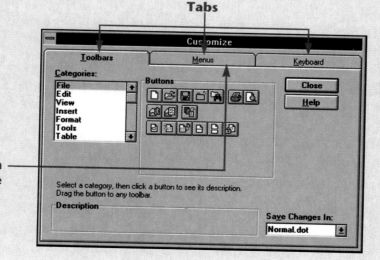

Click here to switch to the Menus page

continues

To Customize Word (continued)

❽ Choose Close.

This action closes the Customize dialog box. To maintain consistency and to avoid confusion while you complete the lessons in this book, don't make any changes to the toolbars, menus, or keyboard now.

❾ Choose Tools from the menu bar.

The second area where you can customize the program is the **O**ptions area. The Options dialog box covers many different areas of the program, offering a broader scope than the Customize dialog box.

❿ From the Tools menu, choose Options.

The Options dialog box displays (see Figure 1.10). You can customize 16 different areas of the program in the Options dialog box. Here again, the tabs along the top of the dialog box let you switch to different pages. Your changes take effect immediately, so they affect the current document and any new document that you create.

Figure 1.10
Use the Options dialog box to customize different areas of the Word program.

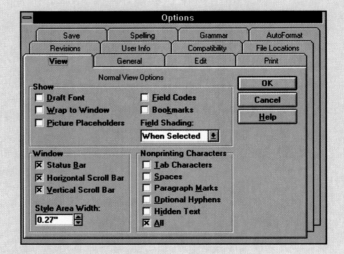

⓫ Click the Cancel button.

The Cancel option closes the dialog box. To provide consistency and to avoid confusion, don't make any changes in the Options dialog box now.

 Using the Customize dialog box, you can customize any of the eight toolbars by adding icons that you use frequently and by removing those icons that you don't use. You can modify the menus to include menu commands that you use often, but that normally require several selections to locate. Finally, you can customize the keyboard with keyboard shortcuts for menu commands, macros, styles, and so forth. By customizing Word, you make the program easier to use, placing the features that you use frequently close at hand.

Lesson 5: Getting Help

By now, you probably realize that you may run into problems as you work with your computer and with software such as Word for Windows. If you find you need a quick solution to a problem with Word, you can use the Help system, a feature of this software. The Help system makes it easy to search for information on the topic that interests you. Word Help also provides examples and demos to teach you the basics of Word.

In this lesson, you use the Search feature of Help to find out more information about margins. Try using Word Help now.

To Get Help

❶ **Choose Help from the menu bar.**

The **H**elp menu displays a number of options available to you when you use Help. Table 1.2 on pages 17 & 18 lists the items on the **H**elp menu and gives you a brief description of each element.

❷ **Choose Search for Help on.**

The Search dialog box appears (see Figure 1.11). The Search dialog box helps you find information on a specific topic.

Figure 1.11
Use the Search dialog box to search for Help topics by keywords.

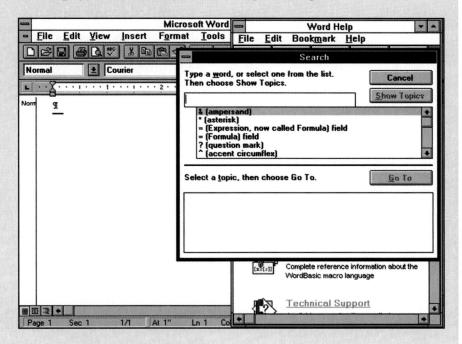

❸ **In the text box, type margins.**

As you type the keyword margins, Word scrolls through the list of Help topics until it finds a match. Now, display a list of Help topics that relate to the keyword.

continues

To Get Help (continued)

❹ **Choose Show Topics.**

Word displays a list of related Help topics in the first list box.

❺ **Choose** `Setting margins with the Page Setup command` **from the second list box (see Figure 1.12).**

Figure 1.12
Choose a more detailed topic from the second list box.

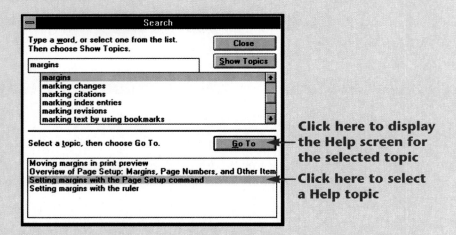

Click here to display the Help screen for the selected topic

Click here to select a Help topic

❻ **Click the Go To command button.**

The Help screen, which contains detailed information about setting margins with the Page Setup command, appears (see Figure 1.13). Note that the mouse pointer changes to a pointing hand when you position it over a Help item that leads to more information. For example, if you point to an underlined word or phrase, the mouse changes to a hand. You can then click that word or phrase to reveal more information. You can also click the Examples and Demos button for a demonstration screen on that topic.

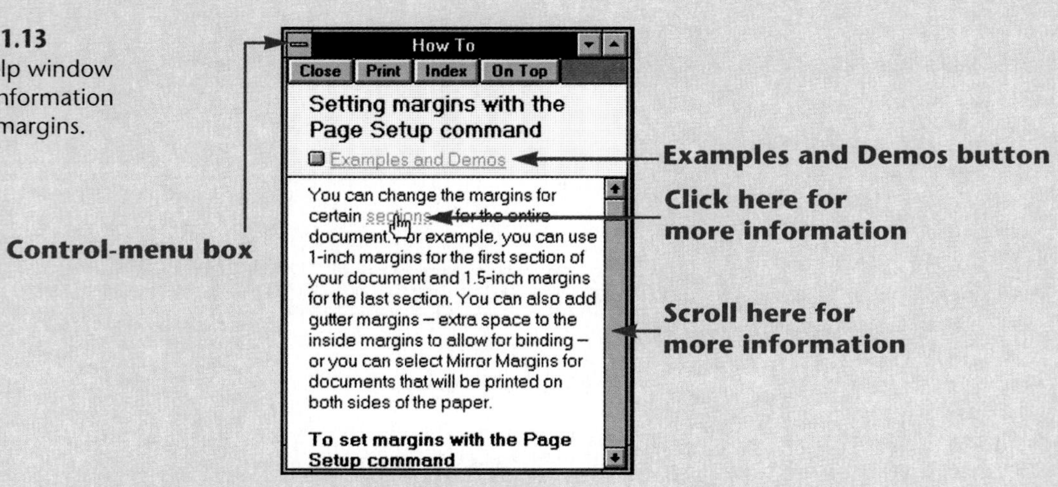

Figure 1.13
The Help window offers information about margins.

Control-menu box

Examples and Demos button

Click here for more information

Scroll here for more information

7 Double-click the Control-menu box on the How To window and again on the Word Help menu.
This action closes Help and returns you to Word. In the next lesson, you learn how to exit Word.

You can use several keyboard shortcuts to get Help. If you are in a menu, you can press F1 to display the Help screen for that menu. If you are in the document window, pressing F1 displays the Help Contents screen. This is sometimes called *context-sensitive* help. If you press ⇧Shift+F1, the mouse pointer turns into an arrow with a question mark. Click any part of the screen with this pointer to identify the feature and bring up the appropriate Help screen.

Jargon Watch

Word provides what's called **on-line, context-sensitive** help. Sounds pretty complicated, doesn't it? Well, this form of help is actually very easy to use.

When you hear that something is **on-line**, that means that it's hooked up to your computer. In this case, that term lets you know that you can get help through your computer, as opposed to through a book or an instructor.

Context-sensitive help means that you can get help about the specific function you are using at the present moment. In other words, if you are in the Open dialog box, you can get help about managing files by simply pressing F1.

Table 1.2	The Help Menu
Item	Function
Contents	Displays the Help Contents screen, which contains the Using Word, Examples and Demos, Reference Information, Programming with Microsoft Word, and Technical Support topics.
Search for Help on	Opens the Search dialog box, which lets you search for a particular Help topic.
Index	Displays a dialog box with buttons for each letter in the alphabet. Clicking a letter displays a list of Help topics that begin with that letter.
Quick Preview	Runs a short demo program to introduce you to Word for Windows.
Examples and Demos	Displays a list of fourteen demos for tasks that you can perform in Word.

continues

Table 1.2 The Help Menu (continued)	
Item	Function
Tip of the Day	Displays the Tip of the Day dialog box, which shows tips on using Word.
WordPerfect Help	Opens a dialog box that lets WordPerfect users select a feature they use in WordPerfect, and then learn how to use that feature in Word.
Technical Support	Displays a list of topics regarding technical support, such as which phone numbers to use and what you need to have ready when you call Microsoft.
About Microsoft Word	Displays Word program release, license information, and system resource information.

Lesson 6: Exiting Word

When you finish working, you should exit Word and exit Windows before you turn off your computer. You avoid losing any of your work by getting into this habit. If you turn off the computer before exiting the program, you could possibly lose some of your data. Complete Project 1 by closing your file and exiting the Word and Windows software.

To Exit Word

❶ Open the File menu, and choose Exit.

If you experimented by typing text into the document window, Word displays a dialog box that asks if you want to save changes to DOCUMENT1 (see Figure 1.14).

Because you were just practicing, you don't need to save the changes. Choose **N**o to exit the program without saving the changes. If you didn't enter any text, the program simply closes.

Figure 1.14
This dialog box may ask if you want to save changes to DOCUMENT1.

Once you have closed Word, the Windows Program Manager appears, as long as no other software applications are running.

If you have completed your session on the computer, proceed with step 2. Otherwise, continue with the "Applying Your Skills" case studies at the end of this project.

② **To exit Windows, open the File menu, and choose Exit Windows.**

Windows displays an information dialog box.

③ **Choose OK.**

Windows closes and returns you to the DOS prompt. When the DOS prompt appears, you can safely turn off the computer.

 You can double-click the Control-menu box to exit any file or program you are currently using. For example, double-clicking the document Control-menu box (next to the menu bar of a document) closes the document. Double-clicking the application Control-menu box (in the Word title bar) exits Word, and double-clicking the application Control-menu box in the Program Manager title bar exits Windows. Again, you are prompted to save any unsaved work before you close any file or application.

If you prefer to use the keyboard, you can press `Alt`+`F4` to exit Windows.

Checking Your Skills

True/False

For each of the following statements, check *T* or *F* to indicate whether the statement is true or false.

__T __F **1.** To open a menu from the menu bar, you move the mouse pointer to the menu name, and click the right mouse button.

__T __F **2.** You can cancel a dialog box without making any changes by clicking the Cancel button.

__T __F **3.** The Standard toolbar is used to quickly change the tab settings and the left and right margins.

__T __F **4.** You can double-click the document Control-menu box to exit Word for Windows.

__T __F **5.** The Formatting toolbar contains all the menu names needed to access the menu commands.

Multiple Choice

Circle the letter of the correct answer for each of the following.

1. The term DOS stands for _____.

   a. Drive Operating System

   b. Disk Operating System

   c. Disk Operational Services

   d. none of the above

2. The correct command you type at the DOS prompt to start Windows is _____.

    a. window

    b. windows

    c. win

    d. run windows

3. Which of the following screen components does Word have?

    a. button bar

    b. command list

    c. toolbar

    d. indicator line

4. A(n) _____ next to a menu command indicates a dialog box appears when that item is selected.

    a. arrow pointing to the left

    b. ellipsis

    c. small filled circle

    d. asterisk

5. The **F**ile menu contains which of the following menu items?

    a. Open

    b. Send

    c. Summary Info

    d. all the above

Completion

In the blank provided, write the correct answer for each of the following statements.

1. To open a menu with the keyboard, you need to press the _____ key plus the underlined letter.

2. Press _____ to display the **Help Contents** screen.

3. The Word _____ feature teaches you how to perform common tasks by prompting you through each step.

4. You can use the _____ dialog box to look for Help topics that contain a keyword.

5. The Minimize/Maximize buttons on the _____ control the current document.

Screen ID

Label each element of the Word for Windows screen shown in Figure 1.15.

Figure 1.15

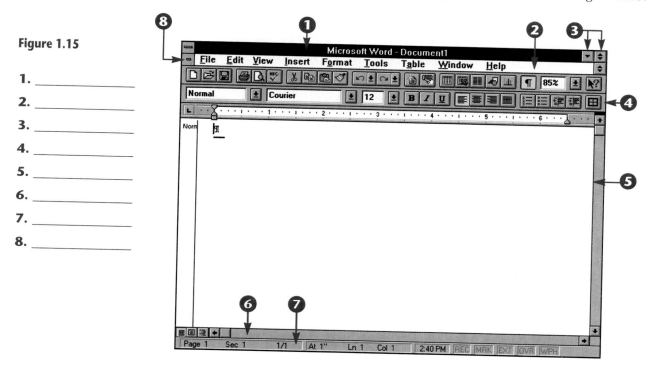

1. _____
2. _____
3. _____
4. _____
5. _____
6. _____
7. _____
8. _____

Applying Your Skills

At the end of each project in *Word for Windows Essentials*, you can learn how to apply your Word skills to various personal and business situations. "On Your Own" case studies let you try using the skills you just learned to create Word documents you can use at home or at school. You can use the "Brief Cases" case studies to learn about how Word can be used in managing a business.

Take a few minutes to work through these case studies now.

On Your Own

Learning About Menus

Now that you have been introduced to the Word screen and Word's Help system, use these skills to continue to explore the program. For this case study, you open several more menus to get a better idea of what features are available and how these features are organized. You also use the Examples and Demos section of the **H**elp menu to see samples of documents that you can create in Word.

To Learn More About Menus

1. From the menu bar, choose **E**dit.
2. Next, choose **V**iew from the menu bar.
3. Now open the **I**nsert menu.
4. Continue opening each menu until you have opened all the menus on the menu bar.
5. Open the F**o**rmat menu.
6. Drag the mouse pointer down through the F**o**rmat menu. Open and close **P**aragraph, **T**abs, Change Cas**e**, and Bullets and **N**umbering menus.
7. Cancel the menus without making any changes.

To View Sample Documents

1. Choose **H**elp from the menu bar.
2. Choose **C**ontents from the **H**elp menu.
3. Choose `Examples` and `Demos` from the **C**ontents screen.
4. Click `Page Design and Layout` from the Word Examples and Demos dialog box.
5. Click `Working with newspaper-style columns` to display a sample document with newspaper columns.
6. Click one of the three buttons shown in the balloons for a brief description of the feature.
7. When you are finished, choose **C**lose; then choose **C**lose again to exit the Examples and Demos screen.
8. Choose **F**ile, E**x**it from the Help dialog box.

Brief Cases

Planning Documents

"Brief Cases" case studies help you learn how business managers and staff use Word for Windows. As you work through this continuing case study, you learn how to set up and run your own business with the help of software such as Word.

If you have already used other books in the Que College *Essentials* series, you have learned how other software applications can help a small, start-up business such as Sound Byte Music, our example in the "Brief Cases" case studies. If you haven't used other *Essentials* books before, imagine that you are the owner and hands-on business manager of Sound Byte Music, a new music store located in a college town.

For this case study, think about the kind of documents you need to create in Word to help run Sound Byte Music. Make a list of all the types of documents you think you will use. Consider all the things you need to communicate in writing to keep your business running smoothly. Note which features of Word you think will make creating each kind of document easier.

Project 2

2

Creating New Documents

Creating a Cover Letter for Your Resume

In this project, you learn how to

- ➤ Enter Text into a Document
- ➤ Save a Document
- ➤ Open an Existing Document
- ➤ Move around in a Document
- ➤ Correct Text
- ➤ Insert New Text
- ➤ Print a Document

Why Would I Do This?

Now that you have become familiar with the Word for Windows screen and the benefits of using word processing software, it's time to put Word to work for you. One of the most common uses for word processing software is creating simple documents, such as letters and memos. In this project, you learn how to create a cover letter for your own resume—one of the most useful letters you can write.

Using the sample information and instructions provided in this project, you work through the steps it takes to enter text and create a document. You can then make necessary corrections, save changes, and print the final result.

Lesson 1: Entering Text into a Document

You can begin entering text for your cover letter as soon as you start Word because a new document titled DOCUMENT1, automatically appears on-screen. For your convenience, DOCUMENT1 provides basic settings for margins, tabs, type style, type size, and paper size. This formatting setup is defined in the default document template called NORMAL.DOT.

For your cover letter, use the document format Word provides; start entering sample text using the steps that follow.

To Enter Text into a Document

❶ Using the steps in Project 1, start Windows and Word for Windows.

Word starts with a new document titled DOCUMENT1. The insertion point appears as a blinking vertical bar at the upper left corner of the document window. You type the text for your letter at the insertion point.

❷ Type the following text:

Your advertisement in The Indianapolis Star for a new marketing associate is of great interest to me. As a recent graduate of the Indiana University School of Business, my degree in marketing gives me many of the skills you seek. I also have a minor in Spanish—perfect for working with your international accounts.

Don't stop or press ⏎Enter when you reach the end of a line. Word automatically moves, or *wraps*, any text that won't fit on the current line down to the line that follows.

❸ Press ⏎Enter twice when you reach the end of the paragraph you've been asked to type.

Pressing ⏎Enter tells Word to go to the next line. By pressing ⏎Enter twice, you tell Word to end the paragraph and then create a blank line between the first and second paragraphs.

¶

❹ Click the Show/Hide icon on the Standard toolbar.

Clicking the Show/Hide icon displays the hard returns you have just entered. When you turn on the Show/Hide feature, Word shows non-printing characters such as hard returns, spaces, and tabs. Notice the paragraph symbol that appears where you pressed ⏎Enter. Viewing the document this way makes it easy to see where you pressed the **Spacebar** and ⏎Enter.

❺ Type the following text:

I believe that that I can be very successful in the fast-paced work environment that you describe, but the only way to find out is to talk with me in person. Please review the enclosed resume and call me at 555-3912 to schedule an interview. I am available to meet on Tuesday and Thursday afternoons.

❻ Press ⏎Enter twice at the end of the paragraph.

Notice that Word inserted a paragraph symbol to show the hard return you typed. Make sure you type the double **that** in the first line—you delete the extra **that** in a later section. After you have finished entering the sample text, check to see how closely your screen matches Figure 2.1.

Figure 2.1
The draft cover letter in a new document window.

Hard return

I-beam

Space

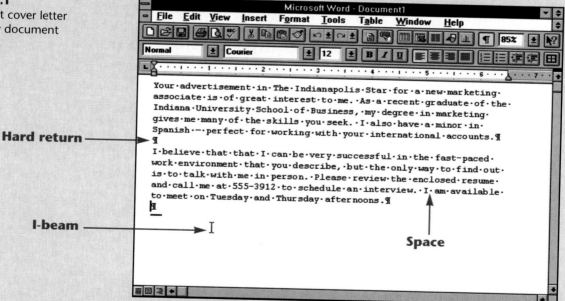

It's wise to save your work from time to time, especially when you have just entered a lot of text. You learn how to save your work in Lesson 2. For now, leave the document open. You will continue to work with the cover letter you created throughout this project.

When you hear people talk about **hard returns**, they may also mention something called a **soft return**. Soft returns happen at the end of every line you type where text is automatically wrapped, or moved down, to the next line. Hard returns are inserted where you want a paragraph to end, or where you want a short line. You insert a hard return by pressing ⏎Enter.

The document **template** discussed at the beginning of this section is simply a set of stored format settings that you can use each time you create a document. If you want every document you write to look like the one you just created, you can continue to use the default template, NORMAL.DOT. Word provides a wide variety of templates for you to use in creating other formats for your work.

While you type, you may make mistakes that you notice immediately and want to correct. You can use ⬅Backspace or Del to remove one character at a time. When you press ⬅Backspace, you delete the character immediately to the left of the insertion point. Del erases the character immediately to the right of the insertion point.

To delete an entire word at once, position the insertion point anywhere in the word, and highlight the word by double-clicking it with the mouse. After you have highlighted the word, you can make it disappear by pressing Del.

Lesson 2: Saving a Document

At this point, you have not safely stored any of the text you entered for future use. At the present moment, your letter is stored in the computer's *random-access memory*, or *RAM*. If your computer *crashed*, you would lose all the work you just finished. For this reason, you should save your work every 5-10 minutes. You can save your work to the *hard disk* (also called the *hard drive*) inside the computer or to a *floppy disk* that you insert and then take with you.

So that you don't lose any of your valuable work (or your valuable time), save your cover letter now.

To Save a Document

❶ From the menu bar, choose File.

Choosing **F**ile opens the **F**ile menu, as shown in Figure 2.2.

❷ Choose Save to display the Save As dialog box.

Because you haven't yet saved and named this document, choosing either **S**ave or Save **A**s opens the Save As dialog box, as shown in Figure 2.3. You can type a file name of up to eight characters, including letters, numbers, and symbols. You can't, however, use spaces in your file name. Now type a name for your letter in the File **N**ame text box.

Figure 2.2
The **F**ile menu.

Click here to save
the document

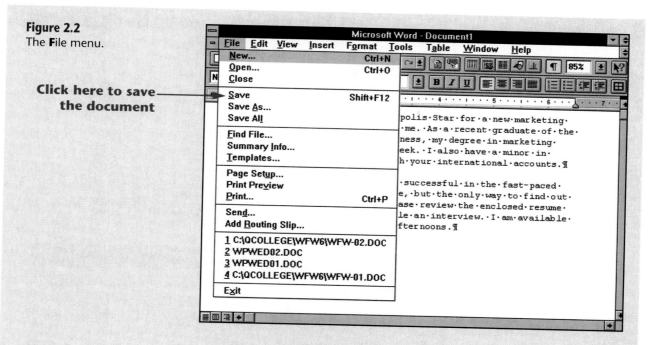

Figure 2.3
The Save As dialog box.

File Name
text box

Drives
drop-down
list arrow

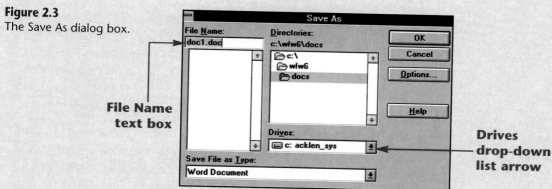

❸ Type coverltr in the File Name text box.

The name you type replaces the default file name (DOC1.DOC) assigned by Word. You can type file names in uppercase, lowercase, or both, but Word automatically converts the names to lowercase.

❹ Click the Drives drop-down list arrow; then click the drive where you want to save your letter.

In the Save As dialog box, Word automatically proposes to save the letter in the current directory on the current drive. If you want to save to a different drive—perhaps the drive containing a floppy disk —choose that drive from the list (see Figure 2.4). If you want, you can also select a different directory from the **D**irectories list.

continues

To Save a Document (continued)

Figure 2.4
The Save As dialog box with the Drives drop-down list open.

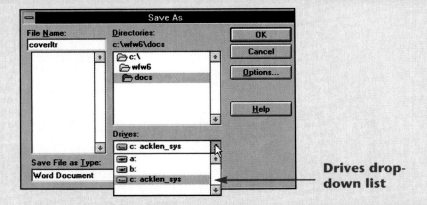

Drives drop-down list

If you have problems...

If you try to save to a floppy disk and you get an error message, check two things. First, be sure you are selecting the correct drive. Many computers have more than one floppy drive. Try selecting another drive and see if that fixes the problem.

Second, be sure you use a formatted floppy disk. If you try to use an unformatted disk, you see an error message that tells you the disk you selected is not formatted. The error message may ask if you want to format the disk now. If you want to format the disk so that you can save files to it, choose **Y**es, and follow the instructions until you have completed the disk formatting process.

Be very careful when formatting disks, and don't format a hard disk drive. When you format a disk, you erase all information stored on that disk. If you have any questions about formatting or about disk drives, don't hesitate to ask your instructor.

5 Choose OK.

This action saves a copy of your letter as a file called COVERLTR.DOC. Word automatically adds the three-letter file extension DOC for whatever name you type—you don't need to type the extension. However, if you want to use another extension, you can type it with the file name. The Save As dialog box closes, and the new file name, COVERLTR.DOC, appears in the document window title bar.

 6 Click the Save icon.

This action shows you the quickest way to save a document as you work. After you save a document for the first time, you can save the document again with the same name, and to the same drive and directory, by clicking the Save icon on the toolbar. If you want to save an existing document with a different name, or to a different drive or directory, choose Save **A**s from the **F**ile menu.

7 Choose the File menu, and click the Close button.

This action closes the COVERLTR.DOC document. In the next lesson, you learn how to open the cover letter document (an existing document) so that you can complete the letter.

Jargon Watch

Once again, you've faced a lot of computer jargon in this lesson. When someone starts referring to how much **RAM** their computer has, don't let it throw you. RAM stands for **random-access memory**, which simply means the temporary storage space the computer uses for programs it's working with at present.

When a computer **crashes**, that term just means that some kind of error—either with the **software** (a program the computer is running), or in the **hardware** (for example, the power supply or hard drive)—has caused the computer to stop working. Everything stored in RAM is lost when a crash occurs.

Again, that is why you need to save your work frequently to a **hard disk** or a **floppy disk**. Floppy disks are the small disks you can carry with you from computer to computer, providing a back-up copy of important information. Even though the 3 1/2 inch variety of floppy disk has a hard outer case, the disk inside is indeed flexible. Hard disks (or hard drives), the hard platters inside your computer, look very similar to the CDs you buy in a music store. Your computer stores the bulk of the programs and data it uses on the hard disk.

Lesson 3: Opening an Existing Document

Now that you have created a cover letter by typing in the basic information, you may want to make some corrections or changes. Before you make any changes or add new text, you need to open the document again.

When you open an existing document, Word opens a new document window, and then displays the document you need. Throughout this book, you open existing documents supplied to your instructor, which you then save using a more realistic file name. Saving the document under a different name lets you use the original, unchanged document at a later time.

Now try opening the cover letter you created in the preceding lesson.

To Open an Existing Document

 ① Click the Open icon on the toolbar.

Word displays the Open dialog box (see Figure 2.5). You can also get to this dialog box by choosing **O**pen from the **F**ile menu.

② Choose the appropriate drive and directory.

Check to see if the COVERLTR.DOC file is listed in the File **N**ame text box (see Figure 2.5). You may have to scroll through the list to find the file. If you don't find the file, it is probably on another drive or in another directory. Make sure you look at the correct drive and directory. This file should appear in the same drive and directory where you saved it in the preceding lesson.

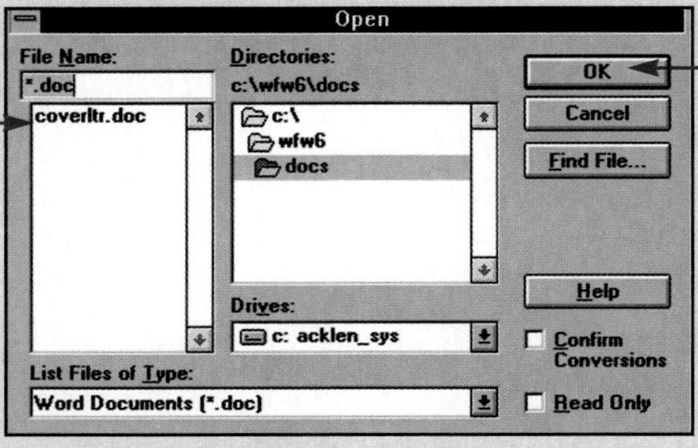

Figure 2.5
The Open dialog box.

Click here to select the cover letter file

Click here to open the cover letter file

③ Click COVERLTR.DOC in the File Name list.

The file name COVERLTR.DOC appears in the File **N**ame text box.

④ Choose OK.

Word places the cover letter in a new document window with the file name COVERLTR.DOC displayed in the title bar (see Figure 2.6). Keep COVERLTR.DOC open because you continue to work with it for the rest of this project.

Figure 2.6
Your cover letter open in a document window.

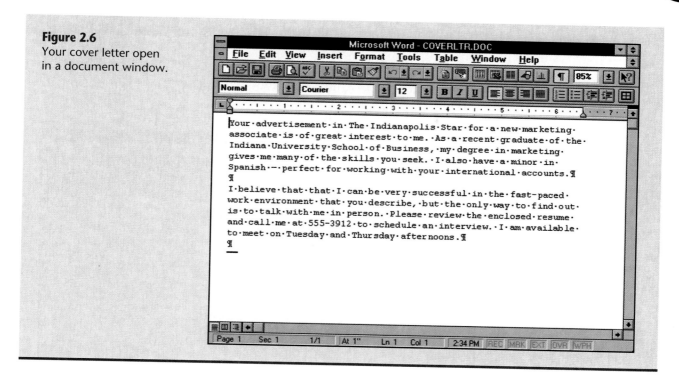

In the Open dialog box, instead of selecting the name of the document and choosing OK, you have another option to open the files. You can simply double-click the name of the document that you want to open in the File **N**ame list box. You can use this technique in most dialog boxes.

Lesson 4: Moving around in a Document

To make changes and corrections quickly and easily, you need to learn the various ways of moving around in a document. For example, you can use either the mouse or the keyboard to move the insertion point in Word. Table 2.1 (on page 34) shows useful keyboard shortcuts for moving around a document.

Your cover letter, COVERLTR.DOC, should be open and ready for work. Practice moving around in the cover letter using both the mouse and keyboard now.

To Move around in a Document

❶ In COVERLTR.DOC, press Ctrl+End.

This action moves the insertion point to the end of the document (see Figure 2.7).

Figure 2.7
The cover letter with the insertion point at the end of the document.

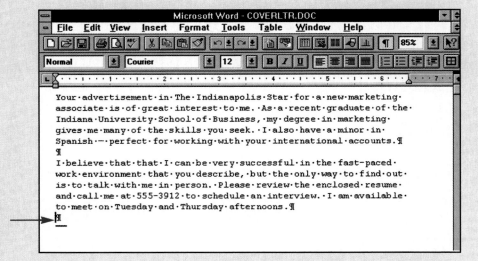

Insertion point

❷ Position the mouse pointer between the 1 and the 2 in the phone number 555-3912; then click the left mouse button.

Clicking the mouse when the mouse pointer is shaped like a vertical bar moves the insertion point to the location you choose. Any new text that you enter or any changes that you make happen there.

❸ In the scroll bar, click the area between the scroll box and the bottom arrow.

This action scrolls the document down one screen at a time to the end of the document—you can scroll up or down in this way. You may be surprised to see that you have a virtually blank document window. Don't panic—you have simply moved to the very end of the document (see Figure 2.8). Keep in mind, however, that the insertion point has not moved. The insertion point remains in the phone number, where you last positioned it.

❹ Drag the scroll box to the top of the scroll bar.

This action scrolls the document back into view. Now, practice moving the insertion point with the keyboard.

Figure 2.8
The end of the cover letter.

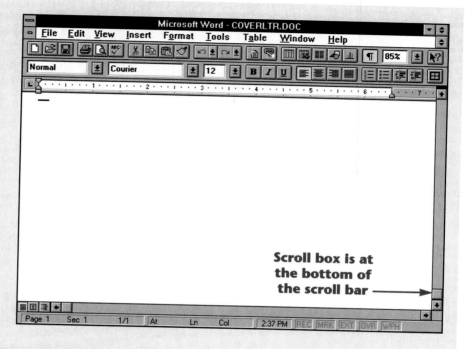

Scroll box is at the bottom of the scroll bar ——→

5 **Press ↑ three times.**

The insertion point moves to the first line in the second paragraph.

6 **Press** End.

The insertion point moves to the end of the line. Compare your cover letter with the screen in Figure 2.9.

Figure 2.9
The insertion point now appears at the end of the line.

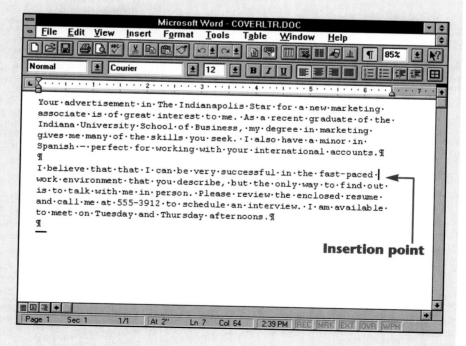

Insertion point

continues

To Move around in a Document (continued)

7 Press Ctrl + Home.

This action moves the insertion point to the beginning of the document.

In most cases, you save your changes to the document before continuing to the next lesson. Because you just practiced moving around in the document (and you made no changes), you don't need to save the document now. In the next lesson, you learn how to correct your text.

Table 2.1   Keyboard Shortcuts for Moving around in a Document

Key	Action
←	Moves the insertion point one character to the left.
→	Moves the insertion point one character to the right.
↑	Moves the insertion point up one line.
↓	Moves the insertion point down one line.
Home	Moves the insertion point to the beginning of the line.
End	Moves the insertion point to the end of the line.
PgUp	Moves the insertion point up by the height of one window.
PgDn	Moves the insertion point down by the height of one window.
Ctrl + Home	Moves the insertion point to the beginning of the document.
Ctrl + End	Moves the insertion point to the end of the document.

You can go directly to a specific location using the Go To dialog box. The quickest way to open the Go To dialog box is to press F5. If you want to use the mouse to open the Go To dialog box, double-click on the position area of the status line (where the current page number, section, and current page/last page are indicated).

Once in the Go To dialog box, you can move to a specific page, section, line, bookmark, annotation, footnote, endnote, or other part of the document using options in the Go To dialog box. Click the Go **T**o button when you have made your selection. See Figure 2.10 for an example.

Figure 2.10
The Go To dialog box.

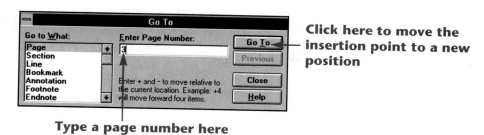

Click here to move the insertion point to a new position

Type a page number here

Lesson 5: Correcting Text

After you read the first draft of your letter, you may decide that you don't like the way a particular sentence sounds, or you may find that you have simply entered the wrong information. Word allows you to delete text you don't want, enter new text, and correct existing text.

You can save a lot of time and effort by changing existing documents and saving them as new versions. For example, once you create a cover letter, like the one for the marketing position in this project, you can change the letter and use it again as a cover letter for different job openings.

Try correcting text now using the steps in this lesson.

To Correct Text

❶ In COVERLTR.DOC, double-click the word perfect in the fifth line of the first paragraph.

The word perfect is highlighted (see Figure 2.11).

Figure 2.11
The word perfect is selected.

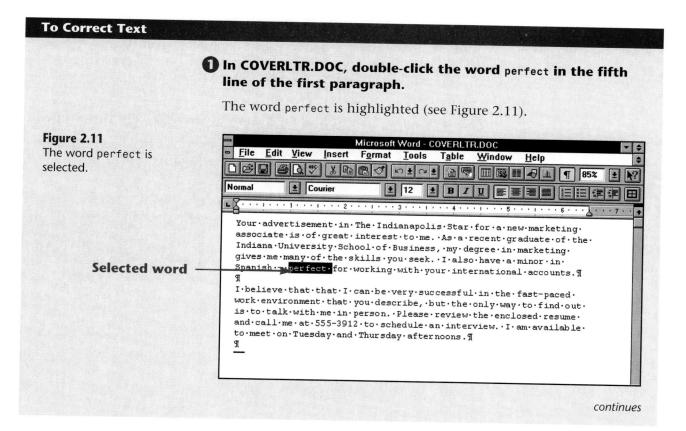

Selected word

continues

To Correct Text (continued)

❷ Press Del.

The word perfect is erased.

❸ Insert a space, type ideal, and then insert another space.

This action makes a slight change in the meaning of the sentence. Don't forget to type a space before and after the word ideal. Notice that the existing text moves to the right to make room for the new text you just entered, indicating that Word is in *Insert mode*. Insert mode allows you to enter new text without the new text replacing (or overwriting) the existing text.

❹ Position the insertion point after the first that **in the first line of the second paragraph.**

This sentence has a duplicate word—that. Delete the first that now.

❺ Press ⬆Backspace **five times to erase the extra** that.

Pressing ⬆Backspace five times erases the word and the extra space after the word.

❻ Press Ins.

Notice that the OVR indicator in the far right corner of the status bar (at the bottom of the document) appears darker. You have now switched to *Overstrike* mode. In this mode, Word overwrites (or erases) existing text as you type in new text when you make a correction.

❼ Position the insertion point before the number 3 **in the phone number near the end of the letter.**

❽ Type 2193 to insert the correct phone number.

Notice that the new number replaces the old number. Be careful not to type over the wrong text when correcting words in Overstrike mode. Compare your letter with the letter in Figure 2.12.

Figure 2.12
The corrected cover letter.

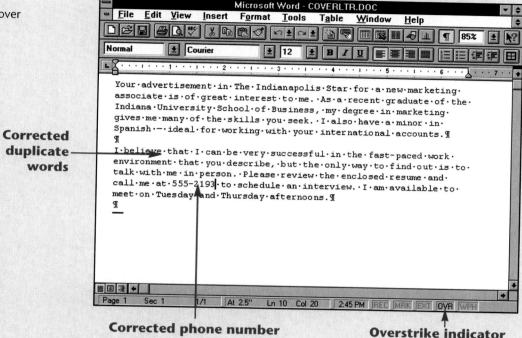

Corrected duplicate words

Corrected phone number   Overstrike indicator

❾ Press Ins **again.**

This action returns Word to Insert mode.

❿ Click the Save icon on the toolbar.

This action saves the changes you just made to COVERLTR.DOC. Don't close this document. You use it again in the next lesson, when you learn how to insert new text.

Jargon Watch

As you just learned, you can switch between **Insert** and **Overstrike** mode by pressing Ins. The Ins key is sometimes called a **toggle key** because it allows you to switch or "toggle" between two different things. When you start Word for Windows, Word uses Insert mode by **default**. A default setting is the way something is automatically done. A **mode** is simply a particular way of doing things.

It may sound impressive to say "Word for Windows operates in Insert mode by default," but that just means Word automatically moves text to the right when you type in new text. If you want to type over existing text, just press Ins.

If you make a mistake as you type, or want to change your text, you can use the Undo icon. For example, if you typed over too much text, click the Undo icon on the toolbar as many times as you need to go back to your original text. To redo those same actions, click on the Redo icon in the toolbar. Click the down arrow at the right side of the Undo and Redo icons to select from a list of recent actions.

Word also has another way of preventing mistakes from happening. Most people make errors when they type—for example, many people type *adn* when they mean to type *and*, or *hte* instead of *the*. Word's AutoCorrect feature detects and corrects these and similar types of errors automatically as you type.

If you want to change the AutoCorrect settings, choose the **T**ools menu; then choose **A**utoCorrect. The AutoCorrect dialog box appears, with a place for you to add additional words you want corrected (see Figure 2.13).

Figure 2.13
The AutoCorrect dialog box.

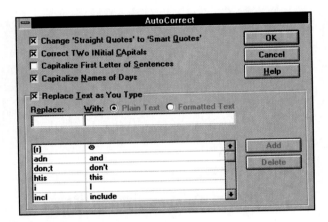

Lesson 6: Inserting New Text

One of the most attractive features of word processing software is the ability to add new information to an existing document. The cover letter you have created is not yet complete. You need to add a mailing address, greeting, and closing to the letter before you can mail the letter.

Try adding this text now.

To Insert New Text

❶ In COVERLTR.DOC, press Ctrl+Home.

This action moves the insertion point to the beginning of the first paragraph (if the insertion point was not already there).

❷ Type June 1, 1995, and press ↵Enter **twice.**

You have just added the date for your sample letter.

3 **Type the following text:**

Ms. Rebecca Keeper
Senior Marketing Manager
Caldwell and Jones
42 Monument Circle
Indianapolis, IN 46260

Be sure to press ⏎Enter at the end of each line you type. Pressing ⏎Enter at the end of each of these short lines tells Word to go to the next line. Word automatically moves the existing text aside to make room for the new text you enter.

4 **Press** ⏎Enter **once again.**

This action tells Word to leave a blank line after the mailing address. Your letter should look like Figure 2.14.

Figure 2.14
The mailing address added to the letter.

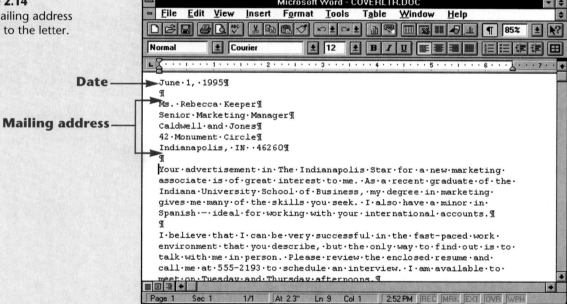

5 **Type the following text:**

Dear Ms. Keeper:

6 **Press** ⏎Enter **twice.**

This action tells Word to go to the next line and leave a blank line between your greeting and the body of your letter.

continues

To Insert New Text (continued)

❼ Press ↓ several times to move the insertion point to the end of the letter.

The insertion point should appear on a blank line below the last line of text in your letter. If you like, you can also use the scroll box to move to the end of the document. Remember, once you have moved to the end of the document with the scroll box, you must click inside the document to move the insertion point.

❽ Press ↵Enter.

❾ Type Sincerely, and press ↵Enter four times.

This step enters the closing of your letter, leaving enough room for you to sign your name after the word Sincerely. Now compare your letter to the one in Figure 2.15. If you like, you can type your name now to complete the letter.

Figure 2.15
The cover letter with the closing.

Letter closing ⎯

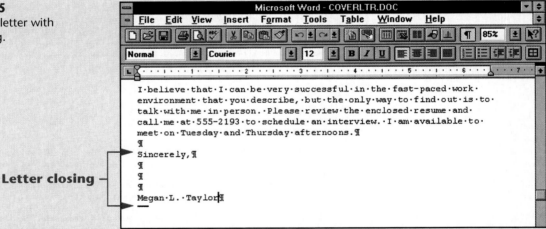

❿ Click the Save icon on the toolbar.

Because this document already has a name and a place on the disk, Word saves the changes to the document with the existing name and location. Leave this document open so you can use it in the next lesson.

Lesson 7: Printing a Document

Now that you have completed your cover letter, you will want to print a paper copy to mail to the employer. You may also want to keep an extra paper copy for your files or to review away from the computer. You should save documents immediately before printing them.

Try printing the cover letter for your resume now.

To Print a Document

❶ Check the printer.

You can't print if the printer is off, if the printer doesn't have any paper, or if the printer is not on-line. Printers often have a light that indicates whether the printer is on-line, or receiving commands from the computer. You receive an error message if the printer is not on-line.

Once the printer is ready to go, you need to check the document you are going to print. Use the Print Preview feature to display the whole page on your screen.

❷ In COVERLTR.DOC, click the Print Preview icon on the Standard toolbar.

Choosing Print Preview displays your entire page as it will look when printed. Your letter should now look like Figure 2.16. This view of the letter lets you see the text spacing and margins so you have a better idea of how the letter looks on the page. Notice that the letter seems to be squeezed at the top of the page. Add some line spacing to improve the letter's appearance now.

Figure 2.16
Using Print Preview to view the entire page before printing.

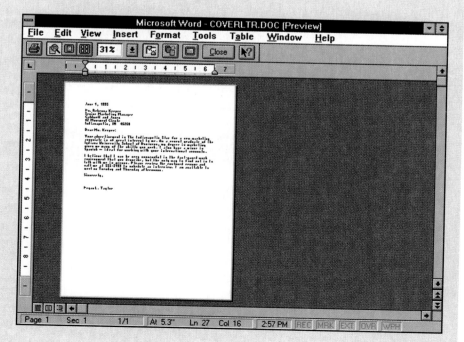

continues

❸ Click the Close button to close Print Preview.

You must close Print Preview to make changes to the document.

❹ Move the insertion point to the beginning of the date.

❺ Press ⏎Enter four times.

You have just added some space to the top of the letter.

❻ Move the insertion point to the blank line between the date and the first line of the employer's address.

❼ Press ⏎Enter four times.

You have just added more line spacing to the letter so that the letter uses more of the printed page. Now, use Print Preview to view your changes.

❽ Click the Print Preview icon on the Standard toolbar.

Compare your letter to the letter in Figure 2.17, and notice the improvement in the spacing on the page.

Figure 2.17
The appearance of the letter is improved by adding space to the beginning and opening of the letter.

Added space —

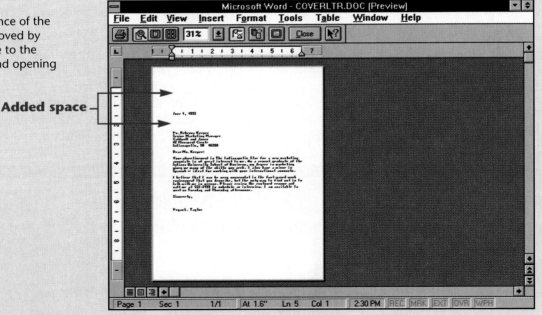

❾ Click the Close button to close Print Preview.

When you are satisfied with your document's appearance, you can then print the document.

⑩ Open the File menu, and choose Print.

This action opens the Print dialog box (see Figure 2.18); you can now choose to print all or part of your document. You can also select another printer, if necessary. By default, Word prints the full document.

Figure 2.18
The Print dialog box.

Type 2 here to increase the number of copies

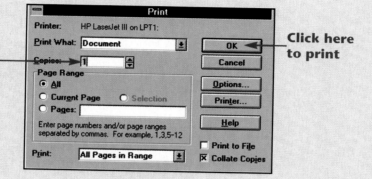

Click here to print

⑪ Type 2 in the Copies text box.

Typing 2 tells Word to print two copies of your cover letter.

⑫ Choose OK to print the cover letter.

Word prints two copies of your cover letter.

Save your work and close COVERLTR.DOC. If you have completed your session on the computer, exit Word for Windows and the Windows Program Manager before turning off the computer. Otherwise, continue with the "Applying Your Skills" case studies at the end of this project.

To open the Print dialog box quickly, click the Print icon on the toolbar, or press Ctrl+P.

Checking Your Skills

True/False

For each of the following statements, check *T* or *F* to indicate whether the statement is true or false.

__T __F **1.** Word automatically opens a document for you when you start the program.

__T __F **2.** You can save your data to a floppy disk, but not to a hard disk.

__T __F **3.** You must format a disk every time you save data to it.

__T __F **4.** Insert mode allows you to overwrite existing text as you enter new text.

__T __F **5.** Ctrl+P opens the Print dialog box.

Multiple Choice

Circle the letter of the correct answer for each of the following.

1. Which of the following can be used as a file name in Word?

   a. MY FILE.DOC

   b. LETTER.DOC

   c. COVERLETTER.DOC

   d. CH.2.DOC

2. The Show/Hide icon _____.

   a. shows the Save As dialog box

   b. opens a new document in Word

   c. displays non-printing characters in a document

   d. closes a document window

3. The Print Preview icon _____.

   a. increases the size of the text when printed

   b. opens an earlier version of the document

   c. allows you to view full pages as they will appear when printed

   d. prints the document

4. Which of the following moves the insertion point to the beginning of a document?

   a. Ctrl+Home

   b. the Undo icon

   c. Ctrl+g

   d. Ctrl+End

5. A document template _____.

   a. ensures that saved information is stored in memory

   b. displays icons on the Word toolbar

   c. toggles between Insert mode and Overstrike mode

   d. creates commonly-used documents with a minimum of effort

Completion

In the blank provided, write the correct answer for each of the following statements.

1. To save a new document for the first time, you click the Save icon to go to the _____ dialog box.

2. You print a document by choosing **P**rint from the _____ menu.

3. The _____ icon displays the document as it will appear when printed.

4. Pressing ⏎Enter at the end of a line of text inserts a _____ return in the document.

5. New text is entered at the _____ point, a blinking vertical bar in the document window.

Applying Your Skills

Take a few minutes to practice the skills you have learned in this project by completing the "On Your Own" and "Brief Cases" case studies.

On Your Own

Now that you have gained some experience in creating and editing a cover letter in Word, you can use these skills to type your personal correspondence. For this case study, you write a letter to your parents.

After paying for your tuition, books, rent, and groceries, you find that you need money to purchase a plane ticket home for the holidays. Write a letter to your parents that explains the increase in your expenses. Ask them to forward the amount you need to purchase a ticket home, and propose a plan for repaying the amount. Let them know that you have found a job on campus next semester.

To Create the Letter

1. Start Windows; then start Word for Windows.

2. Type a draft copy of your letter in the new document Word opens for you when you start the program.

3. Review your letter carefully, checking for misspelled words and typos. Make any necessary changes.

4. Add a date, mailing address, and closing.

5. Save the letter as **MONEYLTR.DOC**, and print it.

Brief Cases

In Project 1, you learned how to find your way around Word for Windows as well as how some of its features can help small, start-up businesses such as Sound Byte Music.

One of the first challenges of launching a small business is publicizing the business. Use the skills you have learned in Project 2 to write a draft of the copy you want to use in several radio spots.

In the ad copy, tell the radio audience that your new music store is now open for business. Let them know that you have a large selection of the latest CDs and tapes, with new releases in all categories of rock, as well as rap, blues, jazz, and classical music. Emphasize that you have a convenient location on East Third Street, directly across from the university campus.

Finally, don't forget to mention that Sound Byte Music also features a popular used CD and tape exchange, with many items in this part of the store priced at half off or less.

To Create the Ad Copy

1. Start Windows; then start Word for Windows.

2. Enter the draft text for the ad copy. Try to be as creative as possible—you need to grab the listener's attention with your ad. Feel free to include additional information.

3. After you have finished writing the draft copy, check the ad for any corrections or changes. Insert a heading for the ad if you don't already have one. Use the editing features in Word to correct the document.

4. Save the final document as **ADCOPY.DOC**, and then print it.

Project 3

3

Editing Documents

Enhancing Your Resume

In this project, you learn how to

> Select Text

> Enhance Text

> Move and Copy Text

> Use the Undo Feature

> Spell Check a Document

> Use the Thesaurus

> Use the Grammar Checker

Why Would I Do This?

I n the last project, you learned how to create and edit a document. You also learned how to insert and delete text, and how to move around in a document. Now that you know some basic editing techniques, you are ready to learn more about editing in Word. In this project, you open a sample resume so that you can proofread and correct the information. Because your resume is one of the most important documents you can write, it's important that it look professional, as well as clearly convey your qualifications.

Lesson 1: Selecting Text

After you have typed a document, you may want to go back and make changes to sections of the text. You use the Select feature to define the area of text you want to work with. Because you can use either the mouse or the keyboard to select text, you learn both techniques in this lesson. A sample resume has been created for your use in this project, so the first step is to open the file for editing.

If you don't have a copy of the student disk, ask your instructor to tell you which drive and directory contain your student data files. You need these files to work through the lessons in this book.

To Select Text

❶ Open the file PROJ0301.DOC; then save the file as RESUME.DOC.

Word places the resume in a new document window (see Figure 3.1). You can now begin editing the sample resume.

Figure 3.1
The sample resume open in a document window.

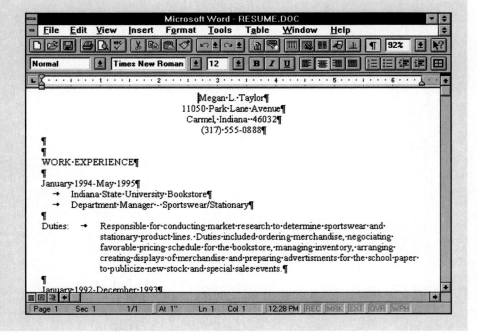

❷ Move the I-beam mouse pointer to the beginning of the name, located at the top of the resume.

❸ Click and drag the mouse down the page.

Selected text appears highlighted (white text on a black background), as shown in Figure 3.2.

Select
To highlight part of the document so the program knows which information to perform the next action on.

Figure 3.2
The resume with selected text.

Click inside the document window to cancel the selection

Selected text

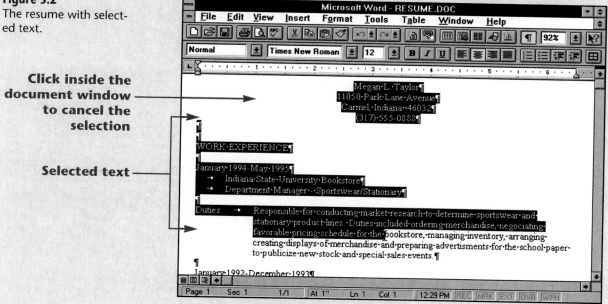

❹ As you hold the mouse button down, move the mouse pointer back up through the page.

Performing this action deselects the text. You can use this method if you accidentally select too much text. If you start selecting in the wrong place, you need to cancel the selection and start over.

❺ Click the mouse pointer inside the document window.

Clicking the mouse pointer inside the document window cancels the current selection.

Clicking and dragging the mouse pointer through text is the fastest way to select large sections of text. At times, however, you may need to select small sections of text. Use the mouse shortcuts to select a word, a sentence, and a paragraph now.

❻ Use the vertical scroll bar to scroll down to the Duties description for the University Bookstore job.

You don't have to scroll down the page if you already see the first line of the Duties description on-screen.

❼ Double-click the word sportswear in the first sentence of the Duties description for the University Bookstore job (see Figure 3.3).

continues

To Select Text (continued)

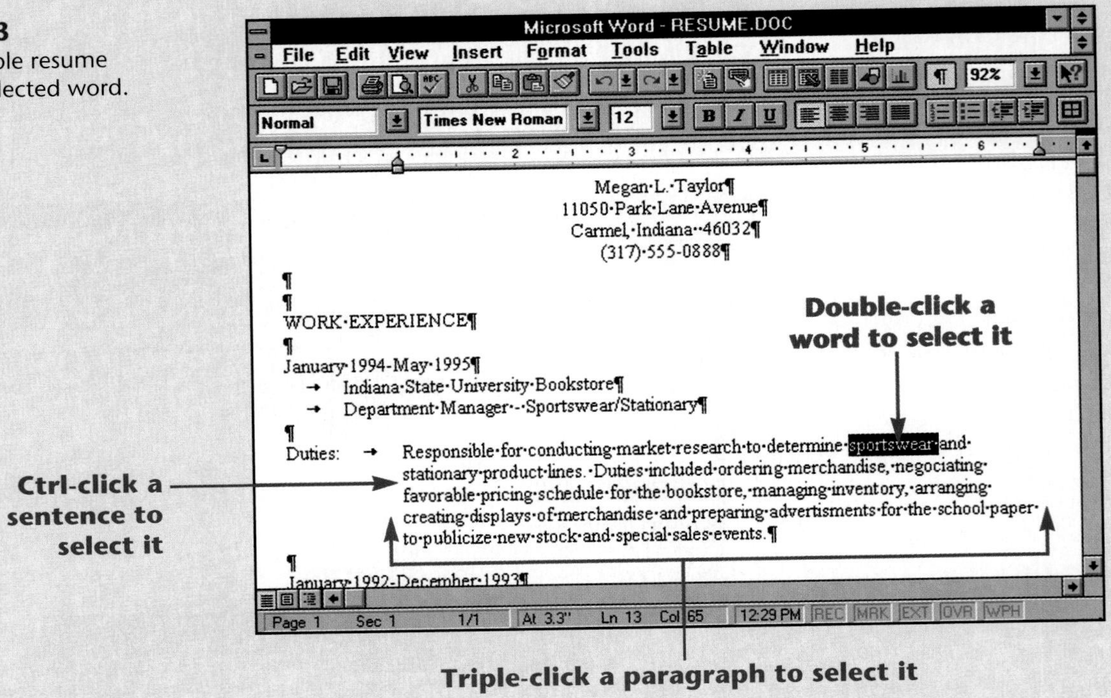

Figure 3.3
The sample resume
with a selected word.

Ctrl-click a
sentence to
select it

**Double-click a
word to select it**

Triple-click a paragraph to select it

The word sportswear is highlighted, or selected. Now, select an
entire sentence with the mouse.

**❽ Press and hold down Ctrl, and click the second sentence of
the same paragraph.**

This action selects the entire sentence; the second sentence should
now appear highlighted. Now practice selecting a paragraph.

❾ Triple-click the paragraph.

If you have problems...

If the paragraph isn't selected, make sure you click the mouse
three times in quick succession and that you don't move the
mouse as you click. If you still have trouble, try one of the keyboard techniques explained in the "Inside Stuff" section.

❿ Click inside the document window to cancel the selection.

Keep the file RESUME.DOC open to use in the next lesson, where
you learn to add emphasis to your text.

You can also use the arrow keys on the keyboard to select text. You may find this method more convenient when selecting small sections of text. First, you position the insertion point where you want to start selecting text. Press ⇧Shift; then use the arrow keys to select text. Release ⇧Shift, and press any arrow key to turn the selection off.

You can also use the left margin area to quickly select text. Move the mouse pointer into the left margin area, and notice how the pointer changes to an arrow that points to the right (the normal mouse pointer points to the left). A single click selects the adjacent line; a double-click selects the adjacent paragraph.

When selecting paragraphs, Word looks for a hard return (or paragraph mark) to signal the end of a paragraph. If you have several short lines (name and address information, for example) that end in a hard return, Word treats each line as a paragraph.

Lesson 2: Enhancing Text

Now that you have learned how to select sections of text, you can add some variety and emphasis to the resume by enhancing sections of text with boldface and italics. Each of the headings should be boldface for emphasis and certain elements can be italicized for variety and readability.

To Enhance Your Text

❶ In the file RESUME.DOC, select the name at the top of the resume (Megan L. Taylor).

Notice that the name and address information is centered between the left and right margins. You learn how to center text in Project 4, "Formatting Documents."

❷ Click the Bold icon.

The name now appears in bold, so it stands out from the rest of the text. Click inside the document window to deselect the name so you can see how the boldface text differs from the regular typeface (see Figure 3.4).

continues

To Enhance Your Text (continued)

Figure 3.4
The sample resume
with the name in
bold.

Boldface text ————————

Click here to
make text bold ————

Click here to
italicize text ————

Click here to
underline text ————

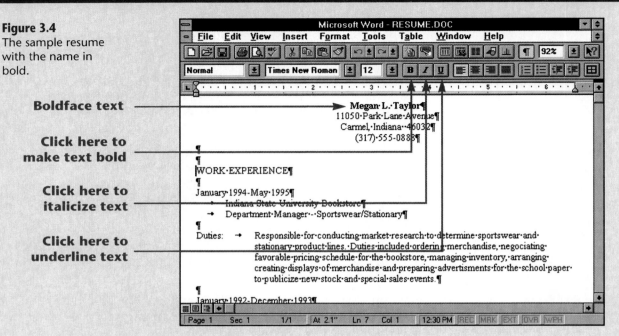

❸ Select each of the following headings and make them bold face: WORK EXPERIENCE, EDUCATION **and** REFERENCES AVAILABLE ON REQUEST.

Each of the major headings should now appear emphasized with boldface type.

❹ Select the dates for the first job description (January 1994-May 1995**).**

❺ Click the Italics icon.

The use of italicized type adds a more subtle form of emphasis than boldface, and is easier to read than underlining.

❻ Select the word Duties **next to the first job description.**

❼ Click the Italics icon.

The Duties heading now displays in italics. To make it clear that the word Duties and all the dates are headings, italicize the other two sets.

❽ Select and italicize the Duties **heading and the dates for the other two job descriptions.**

Your resume should now look similar to Figure 3.5.

Figure 3.5
The resume with boldface and italicized text.

Boldface text →

Italicized text →

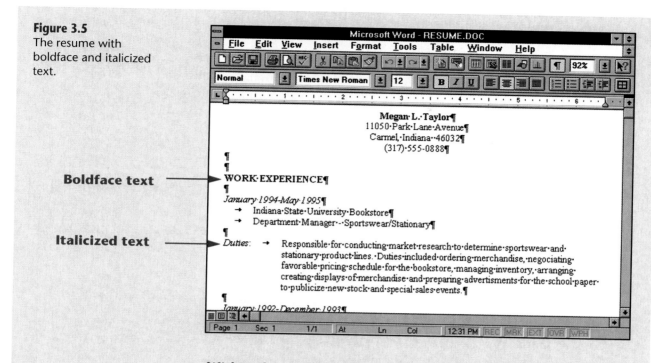

With only minimal effort, you have significantly improved the appearance of a very important document—your resume. Although plain text is neat and easy to read, you want your resume to attract the reader's attention and create a unique appearance that a potential employer will remember.

Save your work and keep the RESUME.DOC file open to use in the next lesson.

The underline icon works the same as the boldface and italics icons, so you can underline text using the same steps that you used for boldface and italics. You might be interested to know the keyboard shortcuts for the boldface and italics features. The keyboard shortcuts are Ctrl+B for Boldface, Ctrl+I for Italics, and Ctrl+U for Underline. To use the shortcuts, first select the text; then press the shortcut keys.

Lesson 3: Moving and Copying Text

After enhancing text, the most important skill you can learn is how to move and copy text. How many times have you written a paragraph and then decided you need to reorder the sentences? What about putting a phrase at the bottom of the page, only to wish you could move it to the top?

Now that you have improved the appearance of the resume by adding boldface and italics to the text, take a look at the content and organization to see if you can make any improvements. In this lesson, you move the Education section above the Work Experience because this order more accurately reflects the most recent accomplishment.

To Move and Copy Text

❶ **In the file RESUME.DOC, select the EDUCATION heading and the three lines underneath it, including one blank line.**

You use the Select feature to tell Word what you want to move or copy. In this case, you want to move the EDUCATION section (see Figure 3.6).

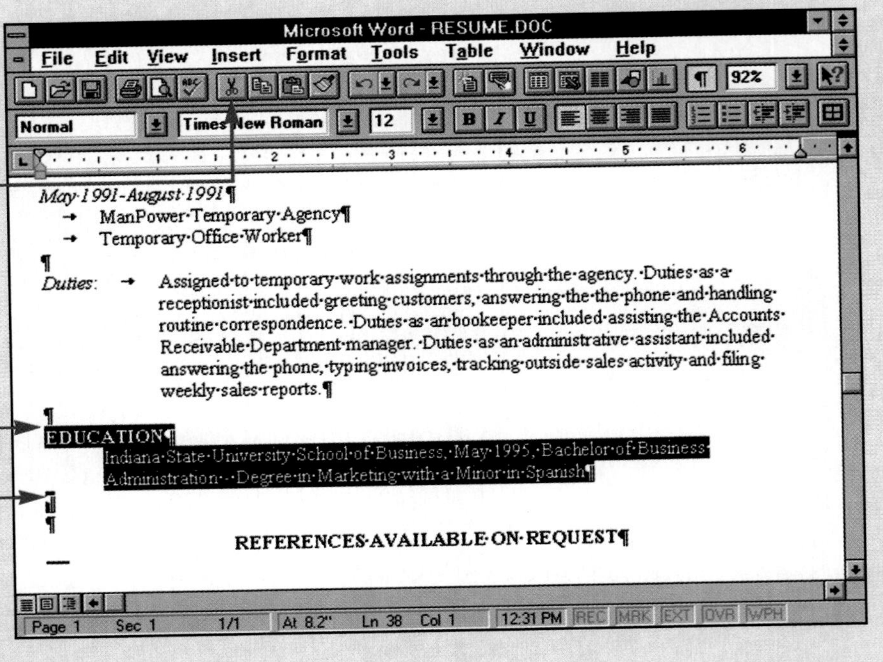

Figure 3.6
The resume with the EDUCATION section selected.

Click here to cut ⎯⎯⎯

Select the EDUCATION section

> Microsoft Word - RESUME.DOC
>
> **File Edit View Insert Format Tools Table Window Help**
>
> Normal   Times New Roman   12   **B** *I* <u>U</u>
>
> *May·1991-August·1991*¶
>   →   ManPower·Temporary·Agency¶
>   →   Temporary·Office·Worker¶
> ¶
> *Duties*:   →   Assigned·to·temporary·work·assignments·through·the·agency.·Duties·as·a·
>   receptionist·included·greeting·customers,·answering·the·the·phone·and·handling·
>   routine·correspondence.·Duties·as·an·bookeeper·included·assisting·the·Accounts·
>   Receivable·Department·manager.·Duties·as·an·administrative·assistant·included·
>   answering·the·phone,·typing·invoices,·tracking·outside·sales·activity·and·filing·
>   weekly·sales·reports.¶
> ¶
> EDUCATION¶
>   Indiana·State·University·School·of·Business,·May·1995,·Bachelor·of·Business·
>   Administration·.·Degree·in·Marketing·with·a·Minor·in·Spanish¶
> ¶
> ¶
>   **REFERENCES·AVAILABLE·ON·REQUEST**¶
>
> Page 1   Sec 1   1/1   At 8.2"   Ln 38   Col 1   12:31 PM   REC MRK EXT OVR WPH

❷ **Click the Cut icon.**

The EDUCATION section has been moved to the Windows Clipboard, which stores the text until you paste it.

❸ **Position the insertion point at the beginning of the WORK EXPERIENCE line.**

You need to position the insertion point right where you want the new section to appear—in this case, before the WORK EXPERIENCE section.

❹ **Click the Paste icon.**

When you paste the EDUCATION section, the WORK EXPERIENCE section moves down to accommodate the new section (see Figure 3.7).

Figure 3.7
The EDUCATION section now precedes the WORK EXPERIENCE section.

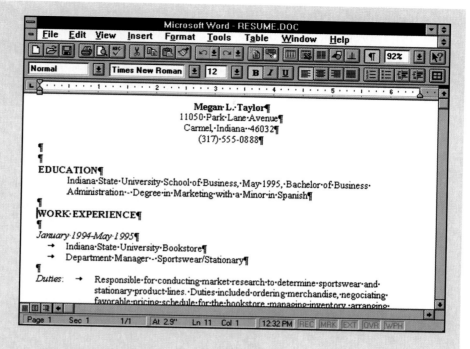

❺ Select the last sentence in the description for the temporary agency.

The sentence describing the experience as an administrative assistant needs to be placed before the sentence describing the experience as a bookkeeper.

 ❻ Click the Cut icon.

❼ Position the insertion point at the beginning of the phrase, "Duties as a bookkeeper..."

Again, because you want to position the sentence about the experience as an administrative assistant (presently the last sentence) *in front of* the sentence about the experience as the bookkeeper (presently the third sentence), you need to position the insertion point *at the beginning* of the third sentence.

 ❽ Click the Paste icon.

If necessary, insert a space between the third and last sentences. The new order of the sentences matches the order of the assignments accepted through the temporary agency.

The sample resume should now look similar to Figure 3.8. Save your work and keep the RESUME.DOC file open to use in the next lesson, where you learn how to undo changes you have made.

continues

To Move and Copy Text (continued)

Figure 3.8
The sample resume with the revised description for temporary office work.

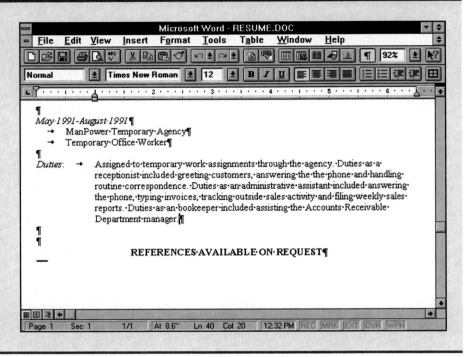

Word uses the terms **cut**, **copy**, and **paste** to describe moving and copying text. (You find each of these commands on the Edit menu). When you cut text, you take the text out of its present location. When you copy text, you leave the text alone—you just make a copy so you can put that copy somewhere else. When you paste, you insert the cut or copied text to a new location.

The Windows **Clipboard** is an area in memory reserved for text that you cut and copy. Because it's a Windows feature, the Clipboard is available to all Windows applications. When you cut or copy a section of text, the text stays in the Clipboard so that you can paste it into a new location. Because the text remains in the Clipboard until you copy or cut a new item, you can paste it repeatedly to different locations.

It's only fair to mention at this point that you use the same steps to copy text as you use to cut text. The only difference is that you click the Copy icon instead of the Cut icon.

Word also offers several text editing shortcuts. First, you can click and drag selected text to a new location. If you click and drag, you move the selected text. If you hold down Ctrl while dragging, you copy the selected text. Of course, you can also use several keyboard shortcut keys. Table 3.1 lists the shortcuts you can use to select, cut, copy, and paste text.

Finally, you can select text and then click the right mouse button to open a quick menu. The quick menu contains the Cut, Copy, and Paste commands so that you can use them without leaving the mouse or having to move the mouse pointer to the menu items or toolbar.

Table 3.1 Keyboard Shortcuts to Cut, Copy, and Paste Text

Shortcut	Function
⇧Shift+Arrow Key	Selects text
⇧Shift+Del or Ctrl+Z	Cuts text
Ctrl+Ins or Ctrl+C	Copies text
⇧Shift+Ins or Ctrl+V	Pastes text

Lesson 4: Using the Undo Feature

The Undo feature reverses the actions that you take on a document. For example, if you accidentally rearrange the wrong paragraph, or assign the wrong formatting command, the Undo feature lets you correct your mistake. Undo works for virtually every action you can take on a document—formatting, deleting, sorting, placing graphics, and so on.

For this lesson, you "accidentally" paste text into the middle of a description; then you use the Undo feature to correct the error.

To Use the Undo Feature

❶ In the file RESUME.DOC, select the section for The Indiana State University Record from the dates down to the last line of the description.

You copy this section, and then paste it to the wrong location.

 ❷ Click the Copy icon.

The selected text doesn't change because this time you have copied text, not moved it. Word has made a copy of the text and saved it to the Clipboard so you can paste the text somewhere else.

continues

To Use the Undo Feature (continued)

❸ **Position the insertion point in between the words** the **and** bookstore **in the** Duties **section for the University Bookstore (see Figure 3.9).**

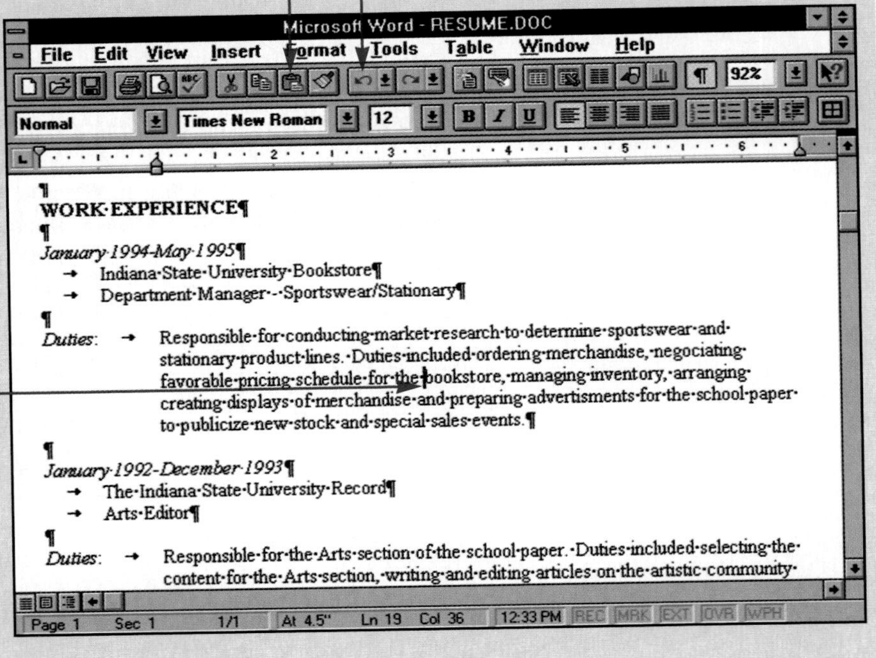

Click the Paste icon to insert the text ———⌐

⌐——— **Click the Undo icon to reverse the action**

Figure 3.9
The sample resume before you paste the text.

Position the insertion ——— point here

```
Microsoft Word - RESUME.DOC
File   Edit   View   Insert   Format   Tools   Table   Window   Help
Normal        Times New Roman   12   B I U
```

```
¶
WORK·EXPERIENCE¶
¶
January·1994–May·1995¶
   →   Indiana·State·University·Bookstore¶
   →   Department·Manager···Sportswear/Stationary¶
¶
Duties:   →   Responsible·for·conducting·market·research·to·determine·sportswear·and·
              stationary·product·lines.·Duties·included·ordering·merchandise,·negociating·
              favorable·pricing·schedule·for·the·bookstore,·managing·inventory,·arranging·
              creating·displays·of·merchandise·and·preparing·advertisments·for·the·school·paper·
              to·publicize·new·stock·and·special·sales·events.¶
¶
January·1992–December·1993¶
   →   The·Indiana·State·University·Record¶
   →   Arts·Editor¶
¶
Duties:   →   Responsible·for·the·Arts·section·of·the·school·paper.·Duties·included·selecting·the·
              content·for·the·Arts·section,·writing·and·editing·articles·on·the·artistic·community·
```

```
Page 1   Sec 1        1/1      At 4.5"   Ln 19  Col 36      12:33 PM  REC  MRK  EXT  OVR  WPH
```

❹ **Click the Paste icon.**

You have just pasted text to the wrong location, and you want a quick way to put things back the way they were. You *could* just select and delete the extra text, but Word offers a faster method.

❺ **Click the Undo icon.**

The **U**ndo command reverses your last action, removing the text you just pasted into the wrong spot.

Save your work and keep the RESUME.DOC file open to use in the next lesson, where you learn to check a document for spelling errors.

If you have problems...

If Undo doesn't remove the pasted text, you probably performed another action on the document after you pasted the text. Any action, such as adding a space or deleting a word, is considered an "action."

Clicking Undo reverses only the very last action taken, which may not be the one you intended to reverse. To Undo a previous action, click the Undo icon again. If you click the Undo icon too many times, click the Redo icon to reverse the Undo actions.

Lesson 5: Spell Checking a Document

Even the best typists and spellers make mistakes every now and then. If you just typed a page of notes for class, you probably don't care how many typos you made. With a document as important as your resume, however, you don't want any mistakes. Word has a built-in spell checker program that you can use to check your documents for misspelled words, duplicate words, and irregular capitalization.

To Spell Check a Document

❶ In the RESUME.DOC file, press Ctrl+Home, and then click the Spelling icon.

The Spelling dialog box opens, and the Spelling Checker starts checking the resume. When the Spelling Checker finds a word it doesn't recognize, it stops, highlights the word in the text, and makes suggestions on how you can correct the word.

In this case, the Spelling Checker has stopped on the word Carmel, the name of a city in Indiana (see Figure 3.10). The word is not misspelled—this word just isn't in the Spelling Checker's dictionary. In this situation, you have a choice—you can ignore the word (here and elsewhere in the document), or you can add the word to a custom dictionary. If you use this word frequently in your documents, consider adding the word to the custom dictionary. If you add the word, the Spelling Checker will not stop on the word when it appears in your documents (unless the word is really misspelled).

continues

To Spell Check a Document (continued)

Figure 3.10
The Spell Checker dialog box.

Highlighted word ───────▶

Not in Dictionary message ───────

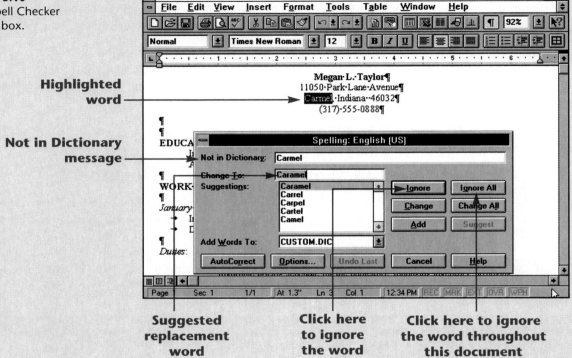

Suggested replacement word

Click here to ignore the word

Click here to ignore the word throughout this document

② Choose Ignore.

The **I**gnore option instructs the Spelling Checker to ignore the word and continue checking the document. The next word the Spelling Checker stops on is a misspelled word—negociating. The program indicates that the word does not appear in the dictionary and suggests a replacement word.

③ Choose Change.

Word replaces the misspelled word negociating with the correct spelling, negotiating, then continues checking the document.

The Spelling Checker finds another misspelled word, advertisments. The suggested replacement word has the correct spelling (advertisements), so choose to replace it now.

④ Choose Change.

The Spelling Checker stops on the next word (ManPower) because of the irregular capitalization. The Suggestions list box contains the word in all lower case, as shown in Figure 3.11. This company name, however, uses the irregular capitalization of the word, so you don't want to choose a replacement. Choose to ignore this word for the rest of the search.

Figure 3.11
Spelling Checker also
stops on words with
irregular capitalization.

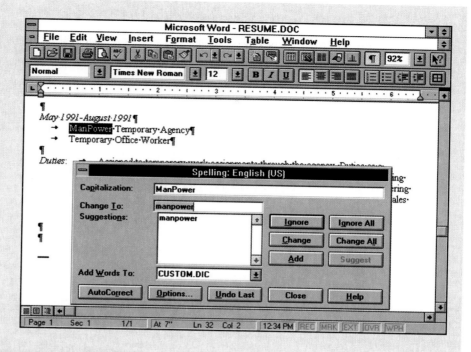

❺ Choose Ignore All.

Spelling Checker stops on the next error, a duplicate word (the the).
Read the phrase carefully before you choose to remove the duplicate
word—in some cases, it is grammatically correct to have duplicate
words. In this case, you want to delete the second occurrence of the
word.

❻ Choose Delete.

Spelling Checker finds another misspelled word (bookeeper) and suggests two replacement words (bookkeeper and bookkeepers). To
select a replacement word, click the word, or use the arrow keys to
move the selection bar to another word. This action moves the
replacement word to the Change **T**o text box. In this case, the correct spelling (bookkeeper) already appears in the Change **T**o text
box.

❼ Choose Change.

When the Spelling Checker finishes, a message dialog box appears
stating that the spell check has been completed.

❽ Choose OK.

Save your work, and keep the RESUME.DOC file open to use in the
next lesson.

If you prefer, you can start the Spelling Checker by choosing **T**ools, **S**pelling, or by pressing F7.

When you start the Spelling Checker, the program checks the whole document by default; however, you can change these settings. For example, if you have to edit a long document and you only want to spell check the area you have made changes to, select the text first; then start the Spelling Checker. You can also spell check a word, which lets you verify the accuracy of the word without having to run the Spelling Checker on the whole document.

Lesson 6: Using the Thesaurus

For those times when you need just the right word to describe something, Word has a Thesaurus program. This program also comes in handy if you discover that you have used the same word repeatedly in your document and you want to find a substitute. The Thesaurus program lists synonyms (words with similar meanings), antonyms (words with opposite meanings), and related words for a selected word. Try using the Thesaurus now.

To Use the Thesaurus

❶ In the file RESUME.DOC, position the insertion point on the word publicize in the last line of the first job description.

This action selects the word you want to look up. You can also start Thesaurus from a blank screen.

❷ From the Tools menu, choose Thesaurus.

The Thesaurus dialog box opens with a list of synonyms and meanings for the word publicize, as shown in Figure 3.12.

Figure 3.12
The Thesaurus dialog box with a list of synonyms.

Selected replacement word

Click here to look up related words for the selected word

List of meanings

List of synonyms

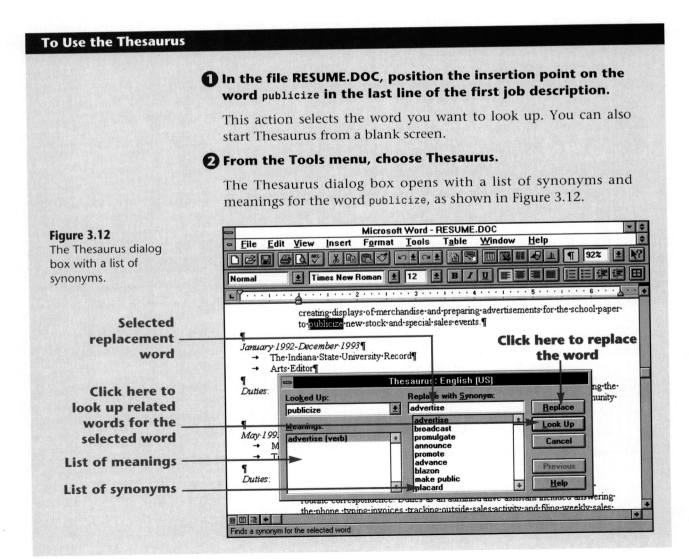

③ Click the word announce.

This action places the word in the Replace with **S**ynonym text box so that you can use it as the replacement word for publicize.

④ Choose Replace.

With the help of the Thesaurus, you have improved the Duties description for the University Bookstore.

Save your work, and keep the RESUME.DOC file open to use in the next lesson.

You can look up more synonymns for a word by double-clicking a word in the Replace with **S**ynonyms list box or by double-clicking a word in the Meanings list box. If the Thesaurus can't find any synonyms for a selected word, it displays a list of words with similar spellings in the **M**eanings list box.

The **M**eanings list box may contain the terms Antonyms or Related Words. Double-click Antonyms to display a list of antonyms for the selected word; double-click Related Words to display a list of related words for the selected word.

Lesson 7: Using the Grammar Checker

The Grammar Checker proofs a document for problems with grammar, style, punctuation, and word usage. This program also offers advice for fixing potential problems.

The Grammar Checker works in much the same way as the Spelling Checker. If the Grammar Checker finds a problem, the program stops, points out the problem, and then gives you the opportunity to fix it. Once you have corrected the problem, the Grammar Checker continues checking the document until it reaches the end. Try using the Grammar Checker on your resume now.

To Use the Grammar Checker

❶ In the RESUME.DOC file, press Ctrl+Home.

This action moves the insertion point to the top of the document where you want to start the grammar check. Note that you can start the Grammar Checker from anywhere in a document.

❷ From the Tools menu, choose Grammar.

continues

To Use the Grammar Checker (continued)

The Grammar dialog box opens, and the program starts checking the resume. When the Grammar Checker finds an error or potential problem, the program stops, highlights the error in the text, and makes suggestions on how you can address the problem (see Figure 3.13). The potential problem appears highlighted in red in the **S**entence text box.

Figure 3.13
The Grammar dialog box.

Potential Problem

Grammatical error detected by Grammar Checker

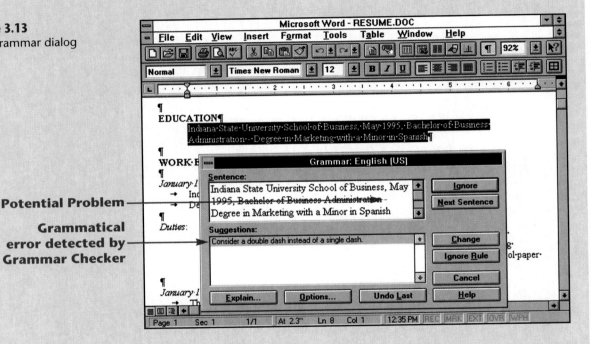

The Grammar Checker detects the first problem in the EDUCATION section and suggests using a double dash instead of a single dash to separate two phrases. Because using two dashes is "grammatically correct" and doesn't alter the appearance of the document very much, change the single dash to a double dash now.

❸ **Choose Change.**

The program finds the next problem in the job title for the University Bookstore position. Here again, the Grammar program has suggested that you use a double-dash, instead of a single dash between phrases.

❹ **Choose Change.**

Now, the Grammar Checker moves on to the phrase with the slash separating two items—Sportswear/Stationary. The advice offered by the Grammar program suggests you should use a word separator rather than a slash. In this case, the suggestion seems awkward, so you can choose to ignore the advice and move on.

⑤ Choose Ignore.

Next, the Grammar Checker stops on the first sentence in the description for the University Bookstore position, suggesting that this phrase may not be a complete sentence. Although the Grammar Checker is correct, most resumes contain incomplete sentences in their job descriptions because being brief is very important. Because the resume probably contains other incomplete sentences, instruct the Grammar program to ignore that particular rule for this document.

⑥ Choose Ignore Rule.

The program has located a problem with an article (an) in the last job description. The Grammar Checker suggests that you replace an with "a."

⑦ Choose Change.

The **C**hange option automatically replaces an with "a" in the document. When Grammar Checker finishes checking the document, a Readability Statistics dialog box appears with a series of statistics about your document. These statistics help you determine whether your document is easy or difficult to read and comprehend (see Figure 3.14).

Figure 3.14
The Readability Statistics dialog box.

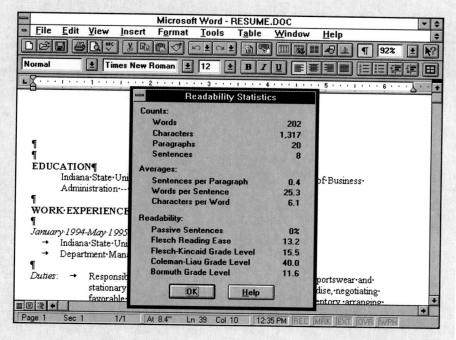

continues

To Use the Grammar Checker (continued)

❽ Choose OK.

This action cancels the dialog box. The changes you have made to your sample resume in this project have improved the quality of this important document. Save your work and print two copies of RESUME.DOC, one to keep and one to turn in. Close RESUME.DOC after printing. If you have completed your session on the computer, exit Word for Windows and the Windows Program Manager before turning off the computer. Otherwise, continue with the "Applying Your Skills" case studies at the end of this project.

The Grammar Checker checks grammar and spelling by running both the grammar and spelling programs, so if you run the Grammar Checker, you don't need to run the Spelling Checker separately. If the Grammar Checker finds a misspelled word, the Spelling dialog box appears on top of the Grammar dialog box. When you have corrected the spelling error, the Spelling dialog box closes, and the Grammar Checker resumes.

Like the Spelling Checker, the Grammar Checker checks the entire document by default. To check a part of the document, select the text before starting the Grammar Checker.

Checking Your Skills

True/False

For each of the following statements, check *T* or *F* to indicate whether the statement is true or false.

__T __F **1.** The Spelling Checker program proofs your document for errors in word usage.

__T __F **2.** Moving a section of text is a two-step process: cut and paste.

__T __F **3.** A single mouse click on a word selects the word.

__T __F **4.** The Grammar Checker checks misspelled words.

__T __F **5.** The Undo feature reverses the last action taken on a document.

Multiple Choice

Circle the letter of the correct answer for each of the following.

1. The Spelling Checker program looks for _____.

   a. misspelled words

   b. duplicate words

   c. irregular capitalization

   d. all the above

2. _____ selects a paragraph.

   a. Triple-clicking a paragraph

   b. Clicking the left margin area

   c. Double-clicking a sentence

   d. Holding down the Ctrl key, then clicking the sentence

3. Which menu contains the option to start the Thesaurus?

   a. Tools

   b. Edit

   c. Format

   d. File

4. In the Spelling Checker, choosing _____ ignores a single occurrence of a word.

   a. Change

   b. Ignore All

   c. Ignore

   d. Add

5. Ctrl+B is the shortcut key for which feature?

   a. Italics

   b. Spelling Checker

   c. Boldface

   d. Undo

Completion

In the blank provided, write the correct answer for each of the following statements.

1. To move a section of text, you must _____ the text first.

2. If you accidentally assign the wrong formatting to your document, use the _____ feature correct your mistake.

3. The Thesaurus displays lists of _____ and _____ for a word.

4. The **P**aste command _____ text at the insertion point.

5. The _____ program uses its own dictionary as well as a custom dictionary that you can add your own words to.

Applying Your Skills

Take a few minutes to practice the skills you have learned in this project by completing the "On Your Own" and "Brief Cases" case studies.

On Your Own

Preparing Your Resume

Now that you have some experience working with the editing tools in Word, you can create your own resume. You can use the sample resume as a guide, but feel free to be creative with the arrangement of the elements in your resume. Use the boldface, italics, and underline features to enhance the resume appearance and make your headings stand out. (The Tab⇄ key lets you indent the company names and job titles under the dates.)

To Create Your Resume

1. In the new document Word has opened for you, type a draft copy of your resume.

2. Go back and enhance sections of the text with boldface, italics, and underline.

3. If necessary, rearrange the elements to best communicate your work experience and unique skills.

4. Use the Spelling Checker to check your document for spelling errors.

5. Use the Thesaurus program to help suggest words that clearly convey your meaning.

6. Use the Grammar Checker to proof your document for grammatical mistakes.

7. Save the resume as **MYRESUME.DOC**, and print a copy.

Brief Cases

Editing and Proofing Ad Copy

In Project 2, you created ad copy to help publicize the opening of Sound Byte Music. After rereading the copy, you see some areas that can be improved. Use the skills you have learned in Project 3 to edit the ad copy before sending it out.

To Edit and Proof the Ad Copy

1. Open the ADCOPY.DOC file, and save it as **ADFINAL.DOC**.

2. Consider changing the order of sentences in the description of the store to place more emphasis on the location than the wide selection.

3. Run the Spelling Checker to check the document for spelling errors, duplicate words, or irregular capitalization.

4. Use the Thesaurus to help find just the right words for your description.

5. Run the Grammar Checker to make sure the ad copy is grammatically correct.

6. Save your work, and then print it.

Project 4

4

Formatting Documents

Formatting a Research Paper

In this project, you learn how to

- ➤ Change Margins
- ➤ Change Line Spacing
- ➤ Change Justification
- ➤ Indent Text
- ➤ Insert Page Numbers
- ➤ Insert Page Breaks
- ➤ Change the Font and Font Size
- ➤ Insert a Header

Why Would I Do This?

Now that you have some experience creating and editing documents, you are ready to learn how to format documents. Word has standard format settings already in place, which allow you to create many basic documents without changing any settings. To create a more professional looking document, however, you can change the standard settings.

Simple changes like different margins and line spacing can make a document easier to read. Page numbers and headers provide important information for the reader. One of the most popular enhancements, changing the font and font size, can improve the appearance of any document.

Lesson 1: Changing Margins

Document margins determine how much white space a document has around the text. You can specify left, right, top, and bottom margins when necessary. Word has preset margins of one inch on all sides, the standard for most business documents, so that you can create many documents without changing the margins.

A section of a research paper has been provided for your use in this project, so open the file to begin editing.

To Change Margins

❶ Open the PROJ0401.DOC file; then save it as REPORT.DOC.

Word opens the report in a new document window. You can now begin formatting the sample report (see Figure 4.1).

Figure 4.1
The sample report open in a document window.

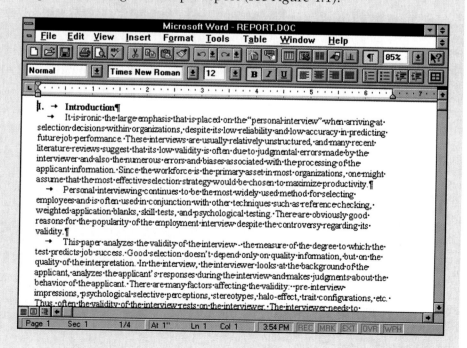

continues

To Change Margins (continued)

② **Choose File, Page Setup.**

Choosing Page Setup opens the Page Setup dialog box, (see Figure 4.2). This dialog box has four different pages—the **M**argins page displays in front of the others. To switch to another page, you click the tab at the top of the dialog box. A sample document page is included so that you can preview your changes before you apply them to the document.

Click the tabs to switch to other pages

Figure 4.2
The **M**argins page of the Page Setup dialog box.

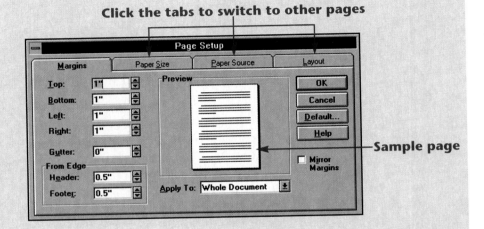

Sample page

③ **Type 1.25 in the Top text box.**

Because the **T**op text box is already selected when you open the Page Setup dialog box, you simply type in the margin setting you want. If you prefer, you can click the up and down arrows to increase or decrease the setting.

④ **Double-click the Bottom text box, and type 1.25.**

Double-clicking the text box selects the current setting so that you can type a new setting in its place. Notice how the sample page changes to show you how the new margins will look.

⑤ **Choose OK.**

The new margins have been applied to the document text and Word has automatically repaginated the text accordingly. Save your work and keep the REPORT.DOC file open to use in the next lesson, where you learn to change the line spacing.

Lesson 2: Changing Line Spacing

As you may have noticed when you created your cover letter in Project 2, Word uses single spacing on all new documents. You can change the amount of spacing between lines with the Line Spacing feature. Try changing the line spacing for the report to double-spacing now.

To Change Line Spacing

❶ In the REPORT.DOC file, position your insertion point at the top of the document.

Before you can change the line spacing setting, you need to select the paragraphs that you want to change. In this case, you want to change the line spacing for the entire document, so you need to select all of the text.

❷ Choose Edit; then choose Select All.

The Select All option selects all the text in the document at one time.

❸ Choose Format, Paragraph.

The Paragraph dialog box appears (see Figure 4.3). This dialog box has two pages—the **I**ndents and Spacing page and the Text **F**low page. To switch to a different page, click the tab at the top of the dialog box.

Figure 4.3
Use the Paragraph dialog box to set formatting for a selected paragraph or series of paragraphs.

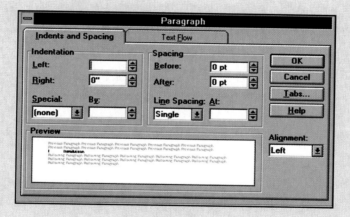

❹ Choose Double from the Line Spacing drop-down list, and then choose OK.

The Double option on the Line Spacing drop-down list sets up double spacing for the document. When you double-space your text, you have one blank line between lines in a paragraph and two blank lines between paragraphs.

❺ Click inside the document window.

Clicking inside the document window deselects your text. The report should now look like Figure 4.4.

Save your work and keep the REPORT.DOC file open to use in the next lesson, where you learn to change the justification.

continues

To Change Line Spacing (continued)

Figure 4.4
The double-spaced report.

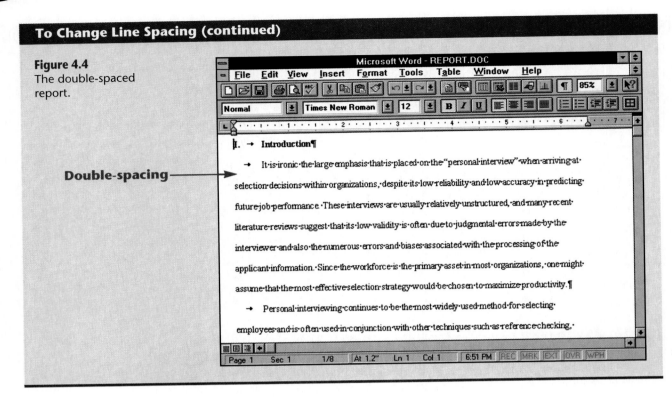

Double-spacing →

If you prefer, you can use Ctrl+A to select all of the text, instead of using the Select All option on the Edit menu.

Word provides keyboard shortcuts for changing the line spacing. Press Ctrl+1 for single spacing, Ctrl+2 for double spacing, and Ctrl+5 for 1.5 spacing.

Lesson 3: Changing Justification

Justification
The alignment of text along the left margin, right margin, or both margins.

Justification describes how text aligns between the left and right margins. Left justification is the most commonly used setting, so Word uses left justification as the default setting. Table 4.1 (page 75) provides a description of the four types of justification.

Now try changing the justification for the research paper.

To Change Justification

❶ Position the insertion point at the top of the REPORT.DOC document.

❷ Choose Edit; then choose Select All.

The Select All option selects all of the text in the document. Now that you have selected the text, you can choose the justification.

❸ Click the Justify icon.

When you click the Justify icon, Word inserts a small amount of space between each character. The text is justified to be flush with both the left and right margins.

❹ Click inside the document window to deselect the text.

The report text should now appear fully justified (see Figure 4.5).

Figure 4.5
The justified report text provides a more formal appearance.

Smooth left margin

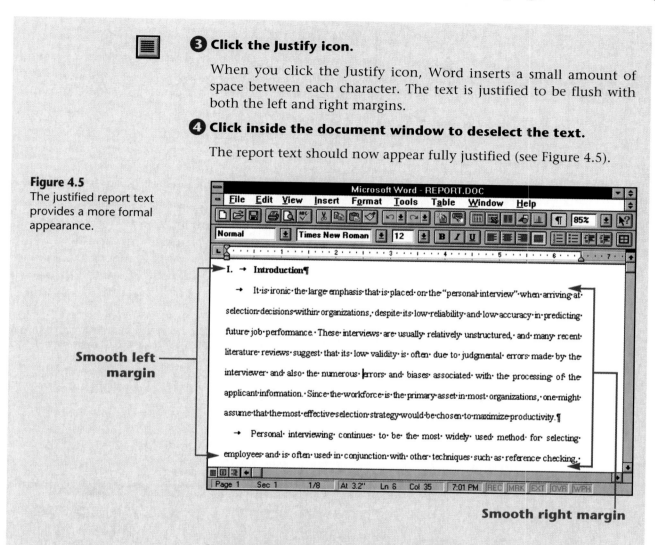

Smooth right margin

Save your work and keep the REPORT.DOC file open to use in the next lesson, where you learn to indent text.

Table 4.1	Justification Options
Option	Effect on the Text
Align Left	Justifies text on the left margin only; the left side appears smooth and the right side appears ragged. The default setting for all new documents.
Center	Centers text between the left and right margins.
Align Right	Justifies text on the right margin only so that the right side appears smooth and the left side appears ragged.
Justify	Justifies text on the left and right margins so that both sides appear smooth.

Lesson 4: Indenting Text

You can use ⎡Tab⇥⎤ to indent (move to the right) the first line of a paragraph. People often use this style in formal reports, letters, and legal documents. If you need to indent all of the lines in a paragraph, you can use the Indent feature.

Don't make the mistake of using ⎡Tab⇥⎤ at the beginning of each line in a paragraph. The paragraph may look okay now, but if you later change anything that causes the text to reformat (add or delete text or change the margins, for example), the tabs move around with the text and end up in the wrong places.

At the bottom of the second page of the research paper, you see a quotation from one of the sources for the paper. The correct format for a quotation is indentation of both the left and right sides (double indent) and single-spacing of the quotation. Try making these adjustments to the quotation now.

To Indent Text

❶ In the REPORT.DOC file, position the insertion point to the left of the word It at the beginning of the quotation:

It is abundantly clear that whatever information occurs first has disproportionate influence on the final outcome of interviews.

This quotation needs to be indented (see Figure 4.6).

Figure 4.6
The quotation at the bottom of page two.

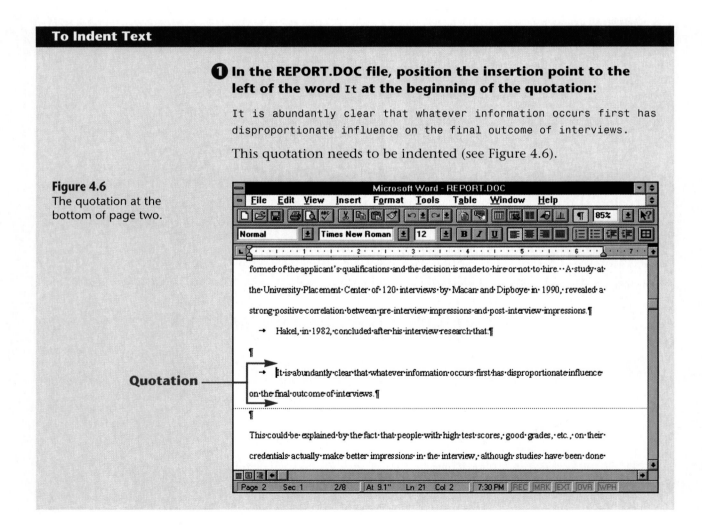

Quotation

❷ Press `◆Backspace`.

Pressing `◆Backspace` erases the tab at the beginning of the quotation. You need to replace the tab with an indent.

❸ Choose Format; then choose Paragraph.

The Paragraph dialog box appears.

❹ Type 1 in the Left Indentation text box; then press `Tab↹`.

Typing 1 sets the Left indentation at one inch. Pressing `Tab↹` moves the cursor to the **R**ight text box and selects the current setting.

❺ Type 1 in the Right Indentation text box; then choose OK.

The quotation is indented by one inch on both sides. Next, you want to change the line spacing for the quotation to single.

❻ Choose Format; then Paragraph.

The Paragraph dialog box appears.

❼ Choose Single from the Line Spacing drop-down list, and then choose OK.

The quotation now appears indented on both sides and single-spaced.

❽ Click inside the document window to deselect the quotation.

The report should now look like Figure 4.7. Save your work and keep the REPORT.DOC file open to use in the next lesson, where you learn to insert page numbers.

Figure 4.7
The short quotation appears indented on both sides and single-spaced.

Indented single-spaced quotation

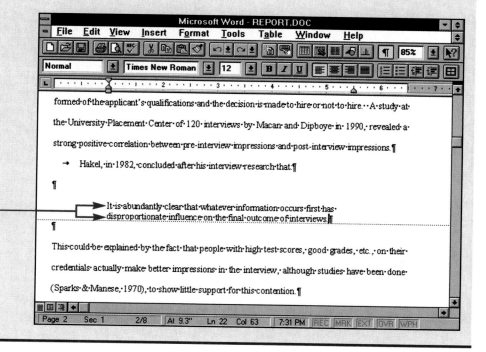

The toolbar has two Indent icons. The Increase Indent icon indents the text from the left side to the next tab setting. Each time you click this icon, the text moves one tab setting to the left. The Decrease Indent icon moves the text to the right by one tab setting.

Lesson 5: Inserting Page Numbers

Have you ever printed a long document, accidentally dropped it on the floor, and then tried to figure out the correct order of the pages? If you have experienced this situation, you already know why you need page numbers in a long document. Page numbers offer a convenience for the writer and the reader as well. In some cases, such as grant applications or research papers for example, page numbers are a required element.

Word's automatic page numbering feature enables you to easily add page numbers to the printed document. Try adding page numbers to the research paper now.

To Insert Page Numbers

❶ Position the insertion point at the top of REPORT.DOC.

You first position the insertion point where you want the page numbering to begin.

❷ Choose Insert, Page Numbers.

The Page Numbers dialog box appears (see Figure 4.8). You can add page numbers to the header region at the top of the page or to the footer region at the bottom of the page. By default, the **P**osition setting puts page numbers at the bottom of the page (the footer region).

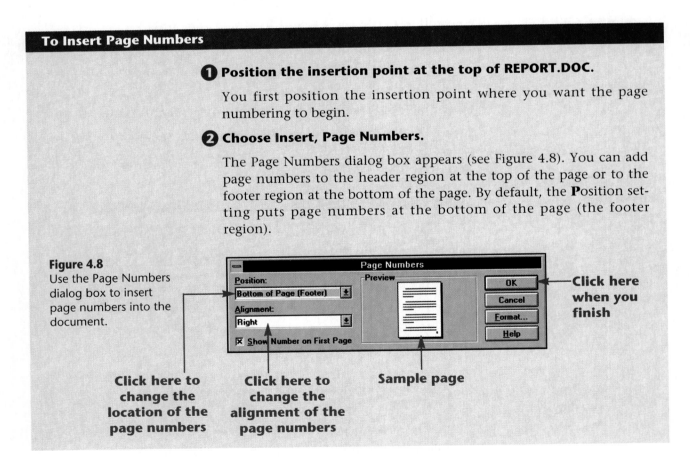

Figure 4.8
Use the Page Numbers dialog box to insert page numbers into the document.

Click here to change the location of the page numbers

Click here to change the alignment of the page numbers

Sample page

Click here when you finish

3 **Choose Center from the Alignment drop-down list.**

This choice centers the numbers at the bottom of every page.

In many cases, you don't want the page number to appear on the first page. If so, you need to click the **S**how Number on First Page check box to deselect the option (and suppress the page number on the first page only). For this paper, however, you do want the page number printed on the first page, so you should leave the option selected.

You can preview the page numbers without printing the document by using the Print Pre**v**iew feature.

 4 **Click the Print Preview icon.**

The Print Pre**v**iew screen appears, as shown in Figure 4.9. Notice the page numbers at the bottom of each page.

Figure 4.9
The research paper is displayed on the Print Preview screen.

Click here to close Print Preview

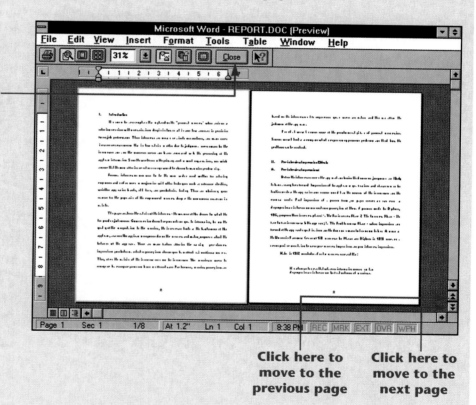

Click here to move to the previous page

Click here to move to the next page

5 **Click the Close button on the Print Preview toolbar.**

Clicking the **C**lose button closes Print Pre**v**iew and returns you to the report in the document window.

Save your work and keep the REPORT.DOC file open to use in the next lesson, where you learn to insert page breaks.

Lesson 6: Inserting Page Breaks

When you have typed enough text to fill the current page, Word automatically creates a new page for you. In certain documents, however, you may want to control where page breaks occur. In such cases, you can insert a page break.

If a heading appears at the bottom of a page, it's preferable to move the heading to the beginning of the next page. You can do this by inserting a page break before the heading.

To Insert a Page Break

1 **In the REPORT.DOC, position the insertion point at the beginning of the second major heading,** C. The Bias of Information Processing.

This heading should appear on the last line at the bottom of page three. Depending on the fonts you have available on your system, the page references listed in these lessons may vary.

Make sure you position the insertion point where you want the page break to occur. In this case, you want the heading to become the first item on the new page, so you need to place the insertion point at the beginning of the heading.

2 **Choose Insert, Break; then choose OK.**

The Break dialog box appears (see Figure 4.10). The **P**age Break option is already selected.

Figure 4.10
Use the Break dialog box to insert page breaks.

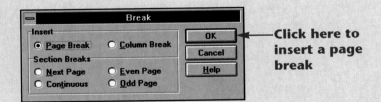

Choosing OK inserts a page break at the point you indicated (see Figure 4.11).

Figure 4.11
A page break displays with the text "Page Break" in the center of a dotted line.

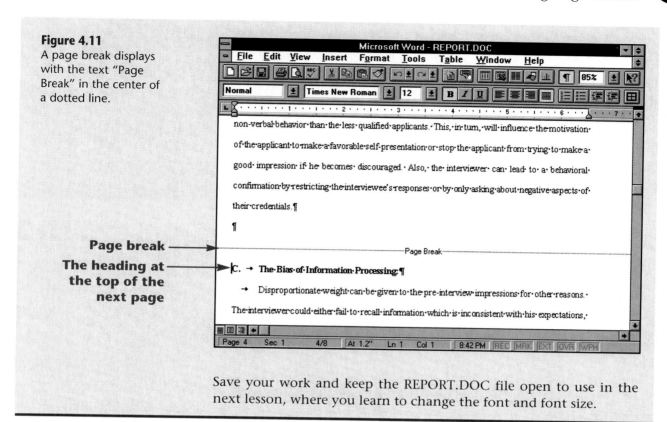

Page break ⟶
The heading at the top of the next page ⟶

Save your work and keep the REPORT.DOC file open to use in the next lesson, where you learn to change the font and font size.

Jargon Watch

When Word creates a new page for you, that page is called a **soft page break**. A soft page break operates much like a soft return, which Word inserts in the document at the end of each line in a paragraph. As with a soft return, you can't delete a soft page break.

As you recall from Project 2, when you press ⏎Enter, you insert a hard return, which forces Word to move to a new line. If you want to force Word to move to a new page, you insert a **hard page break**. Word has a keyboard shortcut for inserting a page break, Ctrl+⏎Enter. Because you insert hard returns and hard page breaks in the document, you can delete these items as needed.

Lesson 7: Changing the Font and Font Size

Font

The style, size, and typeface of a set of characters.

Simply put, a *font* is the style of type used for your text. When typewriters were the primary source of printed pages, the choice of fonts was extremely limited. Now, in the age of processing software and laser printers, you can choose from literally thousands of fonts. You should consider several factors when choosing a font for your document: the font's readability, the font's suitability to the document's subject, and the font's appeal to the reader.

Try changing the font and font size for the headings in the research paper now.

To Change the Font and Font Size

❶ **In the REPORT.DOC, select the first major heading,** I. Introduction, **located at the top of the document.**

This is the first heading you want to change.

❷ **Click the Font drop-down list arrow.**

The Font drop-down list displays the available fonts for the current printer (see Figure 4.12). You can scroll through the list to see all the font choices.

Figure 4.12
The fonts you selected recently will appear at the top of the Font drop-down list.

Font list

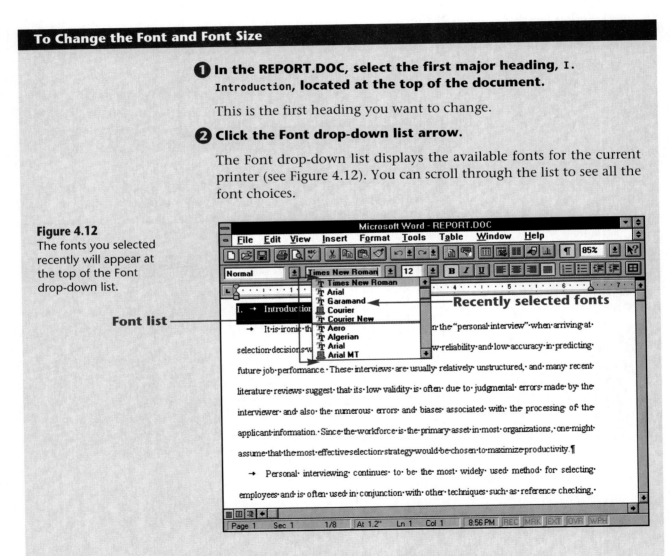

❸ **Click Arial (scroll down the list if necessary).**

The heading now appears in the Arial font, a font often used to set headings apart from body text. While you still have the heading selected, increase the font size to add even more emphasis.

❹ **Click the Font Size drop-down list arrow.**

The Font Size drop-down list displays a range of font sizes. You can scroll through the list if you don't see the size you want.

❺ **Click 14.**

Clicking 14 changes the point size of the heading to 14 points.

❻ **Click inside the document window to deselect the heading.**

Your report should now look similar to Figure 4.13. Now select the other two major headings and change the font and font size for them as well.

Figure 4.13
The sample report with the first heading in a new font and a larger size.

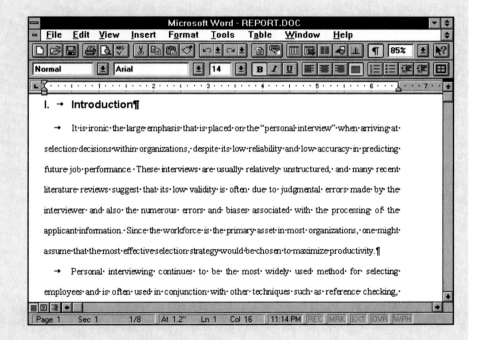

❼ **Select the heading** II. Pre-Interview Impression Effects, **and change the font to Arial, 14 points.**

This heading is located in the top half of the second page.

❽ **Select the heading** III. Perception in the Interview, **and change the font to Arial, 14 points.**

This heading is in the middle of page four. Now, change the font for the subheadings (A., B., C., and so on) to Arial. Leave the size at 12 so the major headings appear larger than the subheadings.

❾ **Select the first subheading,** A. Pre-interview Impressions:, **and change the font to Arial.**

This heading is at the top of page two. The report should look like Figure 4.14.

continues

To Change the Font and Font Size (continued)

Figure 4.14
The major heading in Arial 14-point and the subheading in Arial 12-point.

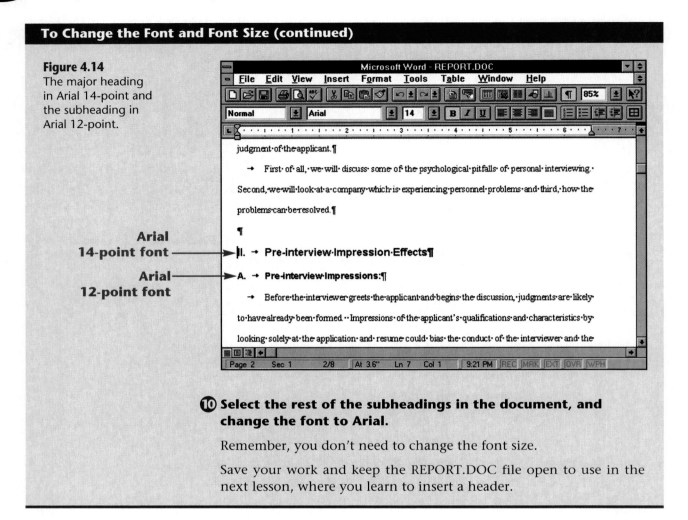

Arial 14-point font

Arial 12-point font

10 **Select the rest of the subheadings in the document, and change the font to Arial.**

Remember, you don't need to change the font size.

Save your work and keep the REPORT.DOC file open to use in the next lesson, where you learn to insert a header.

Jargon Watch

Font describes the size and style of the typeface used in your text. The Windows program includes a collection of **scalable** fonts that you can use with Word. Scalable fonts are available in virtually any size your printer can handle. Font sizes are measured in **points**, a measurement of the font height. For example, a 12-point font is the standard size for most documents; a 72-point font is roughly one inch tall.

The body of the research paper in this project appears in the Times New Roman font, a **serif** font. A serif font has tiny flourishes on each character that help move the reader's eye across the line, making long passages of text easier to read. The headings are in the Arial font, a **sans serif** font. **Sans** means "without," so a sans serif font doesn't have the flourishes. The sans serif font has a cleaner look, which makes it better suited to short blocks of text, such as headings.

If you want to see a preview of a particular font, or if you want to see all the font options in one place, you can use the Font dialog box to make your changes. Choose Format, **F**ont to access the Font dialog box.

WYSIWYG

WYSIWYG, pronounced "wizzy-wig," stands for What-You-See-Is-What-You-Get. This term refers to programs that display files on-screen just as they will look when printed. Because the appearance of a printed document is so important, WYSIWYG is most closely associated with word processing programs such as Word for Windows.

When you make formatting changes in Word, you see the result of your change on-screen as it would appear in the printed document. Most programs today feature some form of WYSIWYG, and some programs (mostly word processors) even allow the user to view the document in different views.

There are usually two or three views, including a draft view, a normal view (usually the default), and a page layout view (displays an entire page). Draft view usually means that the WYSIWYG feature is not applied to the document. Using draft view conserves system resources because the on-screen display is less complex than with other views. The normal view displays the document on-screen as it looks when printed.

WYSIWYG is not confined to word processing programs only. Windows, OS/2, and Macintosh have WYSIWYG technology built-in so that all programs written for these systems contain this feature as a matter of course. TrueType fonts, introduced with Windows 3.1 and now available on the Macintosh, enable the monitor to display text exactly as it appears when printed.

Before the development of WYSIWYG programs, users could not always predict how the output of a document would compare with the commands that they had entered to format the text. A user could accidentally change the font or the font size of text, but not realize they made a change until the document printed. All text looked the same on-screen, regardless of the font it was going to be printed in.

In addition, styles like italics and underlining often did not appear on-screen; they were indicated by a different color of text. Users sometimes had to print multiple copies of a document just to fix character formatting errors that they couldn't see by looking at the monitor.

How Does it Work?

True WYSIWYG is a coordination game between the monitor and the printer. This coordination is best handled by a font manager program, which contains matched sets of screen and printer fonts. Even so, slight differences in the displayed document and the printed document may still occur, depending on how those fonts are created.

If the fonts are bitmapped—stored as a pattern of tiny dots called pixels—the size of the dots vary from monitor to printer, creating a less-than-perfect result. Outline fonts are stored sets of lines, curves, and points, using a mathematical formula instead of a pattern of dots. Unlike bitmapped fonts, outline fonts can easily be scaled to different sizes and proportions. This factor makes it easier for outline fonts to attain true WYSIWYG because they can be scaled to the resolution of the monitor and printer being used.

For further information relating to this topic, see Unit 4A, "Word Processing and Desktop Publishing," of **Computers in Your Future** *by Marilyn Meyer and Roberta Baber.*

Lesson 8: Inserting a Header

Headers let you place document titles, page numbers, dates, and other document identification at the top of every page. Headers are often used in long documents such as research papers.

A header may contain the current chapter and section information, which you can change for each new chapter or section. This information acts as a point of reference for readers so that they can quickly locate parts of the document.

In this lesson, you add a header containing the title of the paper and the date the paper was prepared to the research paper. Try adding a header now.

To Insert a Header

❶ In the REPORT.DOC file, position the insertion point at the beginning of the document.

Position the cursor here so that the header starts printing on the first page.

❷ Choose View; then choose Header and Footer.

Word displays the report in the Page Layout view with the Header and Footer toolbar at the top of the page. The header area on the page is outlined with a dotted line (see Figure 4.15).

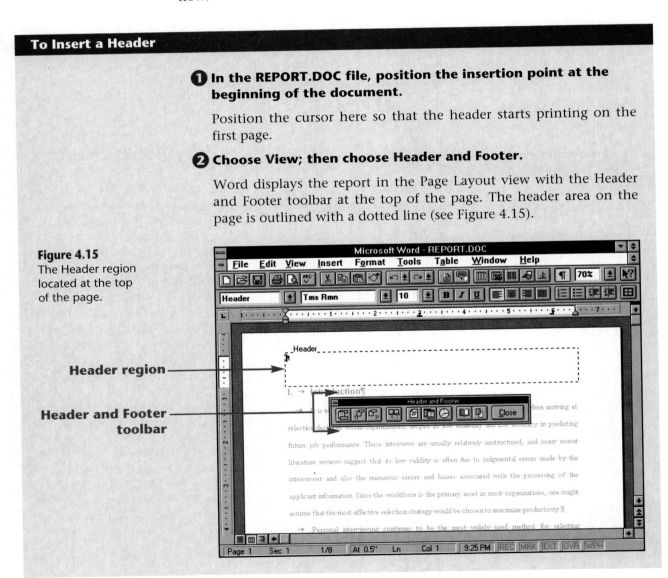

Figure 4.15
The Header region located at the top of the page.

Header region ⟶

Header and Footer toolbar ⟶

To Insert a Header (continued)

❸ Type The Validity of the Employment Interview.

Look at the toolbar, and notice that Word has already selected a 10-point font for the header text. This size ensures that the header does not distract the reader from the body text.

❹ Press Tab⇆ twice.

This action moves you to the right margin so the data will appear flush right.

❺ Type February 1995.

Your report should now look similar to Figure 4.16.

Figure 4.16
The header will appear at the top of every page.

Header text —

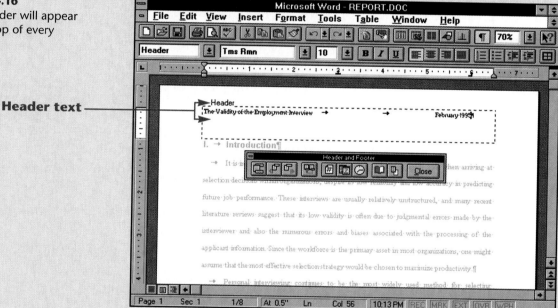

❻ Click the Close button on the Header and Footer toolbar.

Word returns you to the Normal view and clears the Header and Footer toolbar from the document window. If you like, use the Print Preview feature or switch to the Page Layout view (**V**iew, **P**age Layout) to see the header at the top of the pages.

Save your work and print two copies of REPORT.DOC, one to keep and one to turn in. Close REPORT.DOC after printing. If you have completed your session on the computer, exit Word for Windows and the Windows Program Manager before turning off the computer. Otherwise, continue with the "Applying Your Skills" case studies at the end of this project.

When you create a header or footer, Word automatically switches you to the Page Layout view. This view shows you all of the page elements (headers, footers, page numbers, etc.). You can switch to this view at any time by selecting **V**iew, **P**age Layout. Choose **V**iew, **N**ormal to switch back to the Normal view.

Jargon Watch

A **header** is defined as text that appears at the top of every page, and a **footer** is defined as text that appears at the bottom of every page. In most cases, you want the header (or footer) to print on every page.

Checking Your Skills

True/False

For each of the following statements, check *T* or *F* to indicate whether the statement is true or false.

__T __F **1.** You should always select the text to be affected before making a formatting change.

__T __F **2.** The **P**aragraph option on the **F**ormat menu opens the Page Setup dialog box.

__T __F **3.** The Line Spacing feature controls the amount of spacing between paragraphs.

__T __F **4.** The Indent feature moves the first line of a paragraph over by half an inch.

__T __F **5.** You can set page numbers to appear in the header or footer region on the page.

Multiple Choice

Circle the letter of the correct answer for each of the following.

1. The _____ dialog box contains the Indent feature.

    a. Page Setup

    b. Paragraph

    c. AutoFormat

    d. Indent

2. The justification icons on the toolbar _____.

    a. display a drop-down list of justification options

    b. display the four options for aligning text

    c. open the Justification dialog box

    d. center the current line

3. The Page Numbering feature _____.

    a. automatically inserts a number in the center of the last line on a page

    b. inserts page numbers in one of several predefined locations

    c. creates a header with a page number

    d. counts the number of pages in the document

4. A page break is used to _____.

    a. create a new page at the insertion point

    b. create a new page at the bottom of the document

    c. create a new page that cannot be deleted

    d. create a blank page at the top of the document

5. A header appears _____.

    a. at the top of every page

    b. at the bottom of every page

    c. only on the first page

    d. only on the last page

Completion

In the blank provided, write the correct answer for each of the following statements.

1. A _____ contains information to be inserted at the top of every page.

2. The Font drop-down list arrow displays a list of fonts for the current _____.

3. The most commonly used justification setting is _____.

4. Paragraph formatting can be assigned to a single paragraph or series of _____ paragraphs.

5. Word allows you to indent text from both the _____ and _____ sides equally.

Applying Your Skills

Take a few minutes to practice the skills you have learned in this Project by completing the "On Your Own" and "Brief Cases" case studies.

On Your Own

Preparing Your Club's Loan Request Proposal

Now that you have worked with the most frequently used formatting features and commands, you can design the proposal that the Rollerblading Club will send to its loan officer. The club seeks a loan to fund a trip for its members so they can attend the National Rollerblading Convention in Boulder, Colorado. Because you volunteered to act as the secretary, you have to compile the relevant information into a proposal.

To Create the Proposal

1. Open the file PROJ0402.DOC, and save it as **LOANPRP.DOC**.
2. Change the font for the title page. Use larger font sizes for emphasis.
3. Insert page numbers at the bottom right corner of every page except the title page.
4. Insert a header with the name of your proposal and the date you will make your presentation.
5. Change the top and bottom margins to **1.25**.
6. Change the justification to justify.
7. Center the text on the title page.
8. Set the line spacing for the proposal to **1.5**.
9. Select a font and font size for the text of the proposal.
10. Save your work, and print two copies of the file.

Brief Cases

Creating an Annual Report

Use the skills you have learned in this lesson to create an annual report for the investors of Sound Byte Music. The report should include sales figures from fiscal year 1995 and projections for fiscal year 1996. The report should also include future expansion plans, proposed budget figures, and a new advertising schedule. Present this information in an easy-to-read format.

To Create the Annual Report

1. Open the file PROJ0403.DOC and save it as **ANUALRPT.DOC**.

2. Create a striking title page by using an attractive font and larger font sizes.

3. Decide which font and font size you will use for the text of the report, the headings, and the header. Type a sample header and a sample paragraph in the fonts you choose.

4. Create the header with the name of the report and the date you prepared the report.

5. Insert page numbers at the bottom center of the page on every page but the title page.

6. Change the justification to Justify and set up the report to be double-spaced.

7. Create headings for the pages that contain the financial information and advertising schedules.

8. Save your work, and then print two copies of the document.

Project

5

Preparing Long Documents

Enhancing a Research Paper

In this project, you learn how to

➤ Search for Text

➤ Replace Text

➤ Create and Edit Footnotes

➤ Select Topics for a Table of Contents

➤ Create and Compile a Table of Contents Page

➤ Create a Cross-Reference

Why Would I Do This?

Long documents, such as research papers, include special features to make locating information within the document easier for the reader. A table of contents gives readers an idea of the topics you cover in the document. Footnotes provide documentation of the sources you used. Cross-references help make locating information about specific topics easier for the reader.

You may not have to use long document features very often, but when you do have to write a term paper or business report, the long document features of Word provide an easy way to enhance your work.

Lesson 1: Searching for Text

The Find feature helps you locate specific words or phrases quickly and easily. Searching for a word by reading the entire document is often time-consuming and potentially inaccurate, especially in long, complex documents. Word's Find feature searches the entire document and highlights every instance of the word you seek.

You can also use Word's Replace feature to replace a selected word or phrase with a different word or phrase. In the example for this lesson, you find that the spelling of a name cited as a source is wrong. You use the Find and Replace features to locate and replace the misspelled name throughout the research paper.

To Search for Text

❶ Open the PROJ0501.DOC file, and save it as INTRVIEW.DOC.

❷ Choose Edit, Find.

The Find dialog box appears (see Figure 5.1).

Figure 5.1
The Find dialog box.

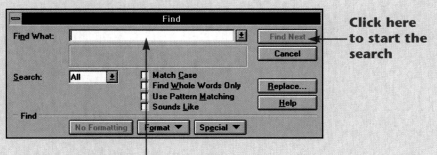

Click here to start the search

Type the text you want to find here

❸ Type Diboye in the Find What text box.

In the text, the correct spelling should be Dipboye. You suspect that this name has been misspelled throughout the report.

❹ Click Find Next.

continues

To Search for Text (continued)

This action starts the search. Word begins comparing every word in the document (including the footnote text) with the text that you typed in the Find What text box. When the program finds a match, it stops and then highlights the word (see Figure 5.2).

Figure 5.2
Word has located a match for the text you typed in the Find What text box.

Search text

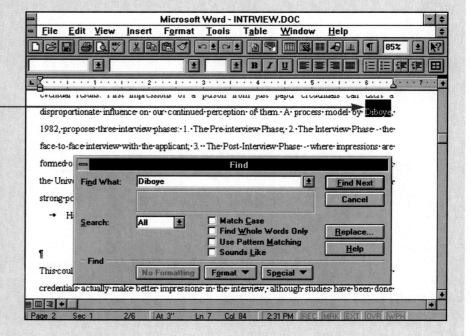

❺ Choose Find Next.

Choosing Find Next continues to search through the document for Diboye. Word searches through the document text, then the footnote text. As suspected, the name has been incorrectly spelled throughout the document.

❻ Choose Cancel.

Choosing Cancel closes the dialog box. In the next lesson, you use the Replace feature to perform a search and replace so that you can correct every occurrence of the incorrect spelling.

Because you haven't made any changes to the INTRVIEW.DOC file during this lesson, you don't need to save the file. Leave the document open so that you can use it in the next lesson.

 If the word you want to search for can be part of another word, the Find feature highlights the larger words as well. For example, if you search for *car*, the Find feature might also stop on *carpet*, *carry*, *care*, and *cart* because these words contain the letter combination c-a-r. Choose the Find **W**hole Words Only check box in the Find dialog box to prevent Word from highlighting the larger words.

Lesson 2: Replacing Text

After you have found the items you searched for, in this case a misspelled name, you want to replace the text with the proper spelling. Use the Replace feature to accomplish this task quickly and easily.

To Replace Text

❶ In the INTRVIEW.DOC file, press Ctrl+Home**.**

This step moves the insertion point to the beginning of the document. You can, however, start a **F**ind or **R**eplace from anywhere in the document.

❷ Choose Edit, Replace.

The Replace dialog box appears. Notice that the Fi**n**d What text box still contains the text that you just searched for—Diboye.

❸ Click the Replace With text box.

Clicking the Replace With text box moves the insertion point into the text box. You type the correct spelling for the name in this text box.

❹ Type Dipboye.

The Replace dialog box should now look like Figure 5.3. Now search for Diboye and replace it with "Dipboye."

Figure 5.3
The Replace dialog box with the information to conduct a search and replace operation.

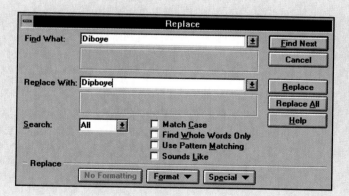

❺ Click Find Next.

Clicking **F**ind Next starts the search for Diboye. When Word stops again on the first occurrence of the word, you can either choose **R**eplace, which replaces this occurrence and then continues searching for the next occurrence of the word, or you can choose Replace **A**ll, which replaces each occurrence of Diboye with "Dipboye" without asking you to confirm the replacements.

continues

To Replace Text (continued)

6 **Choose Replace.**

Word makes the replacement for you and continues searching for other occurrences of Diboye. As with the Find feature, Word searches through the document text first, then the footnote text. When Word stops on the next occurrence, use the Replace **A**ll option to replace the rest of the occurrences in one step.

7 **Choose Replace All.**

When Word can't find any more occurrences of the text, it displays a message box indicating the number of replacements made in the entire document (see Figure 5.4).

Figure 5.4
The replacement message box.

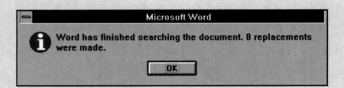

8 **Choose OK; then click the Close button.**

Choosing OK closes the message box. Clicking the Close button closes the Replace dialog box.

Save your work and keep the INTRVIEW.DOC file open to use in the next lesson, where you learn to create and edit footnotes.

You don't have to close the Replace dialog box to reposition the insertion point or to make changes to the document. In case you want to make a manual correction, you can click inside the document, make the correction, and then click inside the Replace dialog box to continue the Replace operation.

Make sure you type the Re**p**lace With text *exactly* as you want it to appear in the document. For example, if you want the replacement text to appear in all lower-case letters, make sure you type the text in all lower-case letters. On the other hand, if the replacement text is someone's name, make sure you capitalize the text in the Re**p**lace With text box.

Lesson 3: Creating and Editing Footnotes

Footnotes provide references for outside sources of information used in a document. You may want to use footnotes in research papers or other types of reports in which you use someone else's work as a source. In some cases and depending on the style requirements of the document, footnotes can be replaced by a reference to the source in the running text of the document.

Word makes creating and editing footnotes easy by keeping track of the correct footnote number and placing each number in the right spot for you. Word also takes care of making sure you have enough room at the bottom of the page for the footnote text.

Footnotes have two parts: the footnote reference number (found in the body of the text) and the footnote number and footnote text (found at the bottom of the page where the footnote occurs). Try adding and editing a footnote in the sample research paper for this project now.

To Create and Edit Footnotes

❶ In the INTRVIEW.DOC file, position the insertion point after the period at the end of the first sentence in the paragraph under the heading The Unfavorable Information Effect:.

You should find this paragraph at the top of page four. If you want, you can use **F**ind to search for this heading.

❷ Choose Insert, Footnote.

The Footnote and Endnote dialog box opens (see Figure 5.5).

Figure 5.5
Use the Footnote and Endnote dialog box to insert footnotes and endnotes in your document.

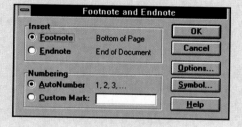

❸ Choose OK.

Word inserts the correct footnote reference number in the text and opens the *note pane*. The insertion point appears in the note pane ready for you to insert the footnote text.

Note pane
The area in a document where footnotes or endnotes are stored.

❹ Type the following footnote text:

Webster, E. C., The Employment Interview: A Social Judgment Process. Schomberg, Ontario, Canada: SIP. 1982.

Your document should now look like Figure 5.6.

continues

To Create and Edit Footnotes (continued)

Footnote number in the text

Figure 5.6
The new footnote shown in the note pane.

Note pane

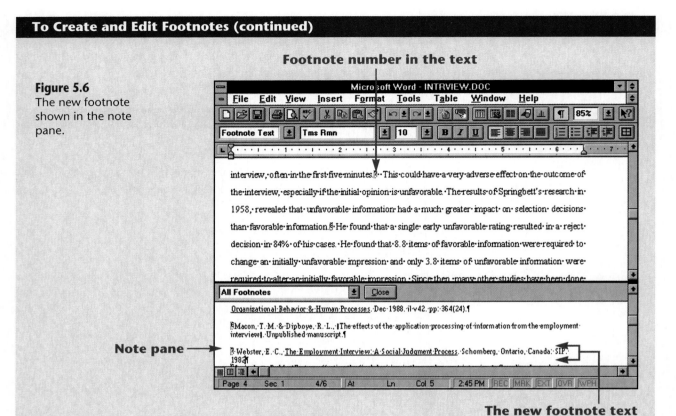

The new footnote text

5 **Move to the top of the note pane by clicking the up scroll arrow.**

You need to edit the first footnote, which appears at the top of the note pane.

6 **Select the text** Academy of Management Review 7.

This publication reference needs to be underlined to fit the style conventions of the research paper example.

7 **Click the Underline icon.**

This action underlines the selected text. Your document should now look like Figure 5.7.

Figure 5.7
The publication reference in the first footnote should be underlined.

Close the note pane ⎯

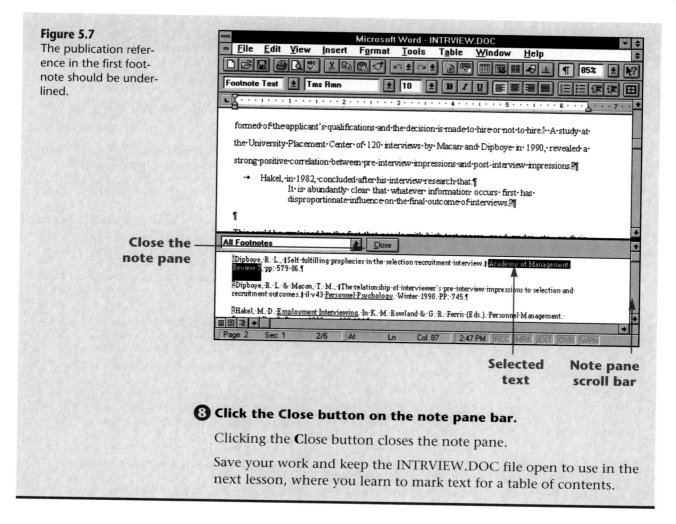

Selected text   Note pane scroll bar

❽ **Click the Close button on the note pane bar.**

Clicking the **C**lose button closes the note pane.

Save your work and keep the INTRVIEW.DOC file open to use in the next lesson, where you learn to mark text for a table of contents.

When you need to work with a lot of footnotes, you may want to adjust the Zoom setting so you can see the footnote numbers and footnote text more clearly. In the text, footnote numbers appear surrounded by a dotted line, which can make the numbers difficult to read.

Working with endnotes in Word is essentially the same as working with footnotes—endnotes just appear on a separate page at the end of the document.

Word Processing—A Pain in the Back

Is using word processing software such as Word for Windows a pleasure or a pain? Some people who work long hours at word processing might say it's a pain in the back... or wrist, or eyes.

Ergonomics is the science that studies how to best create a comfortable and safe working environment, which allows people to be productive without experiencing pain. The ergonomics of using a computer has recently become a major concern, mainly because people who were used to springy typewriter keys and manual carriage returns started to experience wrist and hand pain when using their computers.

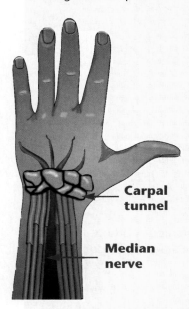

Carpal tunnel

Median nerve

The cause of the pain eventually became apparent: people were holding their wrists at unnatural angles for extended period of time without breaks. The pain is caused by pressure on the median nerve, a nerve that runs through the carpal tunnel of the wrist. (The carpal tunnel is a circle of eight bones in the wrist through which nerves and tendons run to the hand.) When the nerve is pinched, the individual can experience numbness, tingling, and pain in the fingers. This condition, called Carpal Tunnel Syndrome (CTS), has become increasingly common in people who spend hours typing long documents using keyboards.

Carpal Tunnel Syn-drome has recently been compared to other repetitive stress injuries (RSIs), which until now were mainly associated with factory workers and people whose jobs require them to perform the same action repeatedly. RSI is not a new phenomenon; it already costs about $7 billion a year from lost worker productivity and medical costs. With more and morepeople developing Carpal Tunnel Syndrome, that number will probably skyrocket—unless employers can improve the work environments.

Simple equipment improvements that can help improve the ergonomics of a computer include:

Wrist rest. A small foam-covered, shelf-like unit placed in front of a keyboard on which the typist can rest his/her wrists. A wrist rest helps to ensure that the wrists remain flat (parallel to the floor), which reduces the risk of Carpal Tunnel Syndrome.

Adjustable keyboards. Many keyboard manufacturers have developed more ergonomically correct keyboards. Some of these keyboards have adjustable sections so the worker can position the keys at a more comfortable level. Other "keyboards" have eliminated keys altogether: they rely on finger pressure instead of hand movement.

Adjustable keyboard drawers. A tabletop is very rarely the ideal position for a keyboard. The keyboard should be on a special shelf or drawer that can be adjusted for each individual user.

Monitor stands and glare guards. To avoid unnecessary eye strain, the monitor should be at eye level or slightly lower. If glare becomes a problem, there are several glare guards on the market that help reduce eyestrain.

Adjustable chairs. A good chair allows a person to adjust not only the height, but also the backrest and armrests. A chair that can be adjusted to promote good posture reduces stress on the lower back.

In addition to ergonomic changes in furniture and posture, computer users should take frequent breaks to avoid RSI. Experts recommend a ten minute break every hour. That doesn't mean that the user has to stop working ten minutes out of every hour, it just means that people should stop using the computer for ten minutes and focus their attention on other tasks. Focusing the eyes on something else also relieves eyestrain. It is also important to move around often. A worker should not sit in the same position for a long time.

For further information relating to this topic, see Unit 8A, "Ergonomics," of **Computers in Your Future** *by Marilyn Meyer and Roberta Baber.*

Lesson 4: Selecting Topics for a Table of Contents

A table of contents provides readers with a guide to the topics covered in a long document. Word makes creating a table of contents easy—all you have to do is select the text that you want to appear in the table of contents, assign a heading style, and then compile the table. Word then builds the table of contents for you.

When you make editing changes to the document, you need to recompile the table of contents so that Word can update the page numbers. In this lesson, try creating a table of contents that lists all of the headings and sub-headings in the research paper.

To Select Topics for a Table of Contents

❶ In the INTRVIEW.DOC file, select Introduction, the first heading.

Make sure you only select the text, and not the paragraph mark after it (see Figure 5.8). If you include the paragraph mark, it appears in the table of contents as an extra line. The Table of Contents feature automatically includes a blank line between entries.

Click here to select a heading style

Figure 5.8
The interview report with a selected heading.

Select this heading

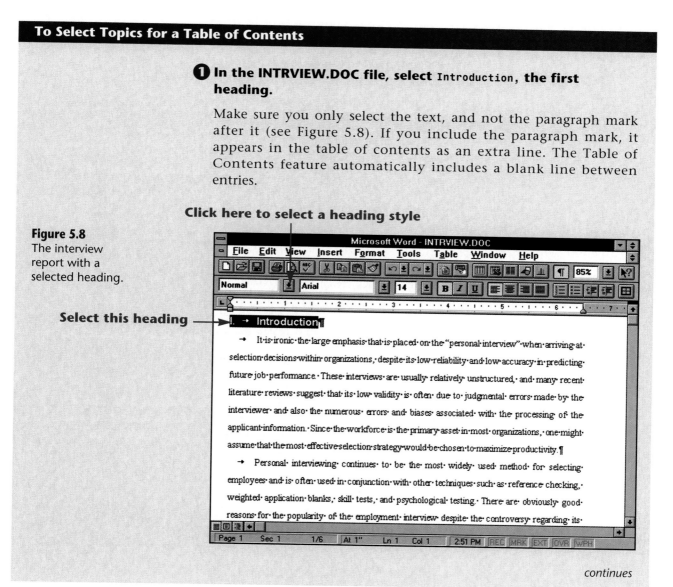

continues

To Select Topics for a Table of Contents (continued)

If you have problems...

If you click the selection area or triple-click the heading, Word includes the paragraph mark after the heading in the selection. You may find that the easiest way to select only the heading is to start at the end of the heading, and then click and drag to the left until you select the heading.

2 Click the Style drop-down list arrow.

Clicking the drop-down list arrow displays a list of Word styles. At this point, the document text and headings have the style Normal.

3 Select the Heading 1 style from the Style drop-down list.

You may have to scroll through the list of styles to see the Heading 1 style.

4 Select the heading Pre-interview Impression Effects.

Because this heading is the second major heading in the report, it should have a style of Heading 1 as well.

5 Click the Style drop-down list arrow, and select Heading 1.

The next heading is a subheading under a major heading, so it should be assigned a style of Heading 2.

6 Select the subheading Pre-interview Impressions.

When you select the text, make sure you don't include the colon at the end of the heading; otherwise, the colon shows up in the table of contents. Also, remember to only select the text of the heading, not the paragraph mark after the text.

7 Click the Style drop-down list arrow, and select Heading 2.

The Heading 2 style uses italics to set the subheadings apart from the major headings.

8 Select the rest of the headings and subheadings in the document; give the major headings (with Roman numerals) the Heading 1 style and the subheadings (with letters) the Heading 2 style.

Marking the rest of the entries completes the preparation for creating the table of contents. Save your work and keep the INTRVIEW.DOC file open for the next lesson, where you learn to create and compile a table of contents page.

Lesson 5: Creating and Compiling a Table of Contents Page

After you have selected the topics you want to appear in the table of contents, you need to create a separate page for the table. Typically, a table of contents appears by itself on a page preceding the body of the research paper.

In this lesson, you create a new page for the table of contents, and then add a heading for the table of contents page. Word provides a selection of format templates for you to use in creating the table. After you choose the format, Word compiles the table of contents using the topics you selected.

To Create and Compile a Table of Contents Page

❶ In the INTRVIEW.DOC file, press Ctrl + Home.

This action positions the insertion point at the beginning of the document.

❷ Press Ctrl + ⏎Enter; **then press** ↑.

Pressing Ctrl + ⏎Enter inserts a page break. Pressing the ↑ moves the insertion point into the new page you just created.

❸ Press ⏎Enter **once; then press** ↑.

Pressing ⏎Enter creates a blank line for the title, and pressing the ↑ moves you to that line. Now, you need to type the title for the table.

❹ Click the Center icon.

Clicking the Center icon moves the insertion point to the middle of the page so that you can type a centered title.

❺ Type Table of Contents; then press ⏎Enter **twice.**

You inserted a blank line between the title and the page number heading.

❻ Click the Align Right icon.

Clicking the Align Right icon moves the insertion point to the right margin so that any text you enter aligns flush right.

❼ Type Page; then press ⏎Enter **twice.**

The Page heading appears flush right.

❽ Click the Align Left icon.

Clicking the Align Left icon moves the insertion point to the left margin so that the table of contents entries align flush left. The Table of Contents page should now look like Figure 5.9. You can now have Word compile the table of contents.

❾ Choose Insert, Index and Tables.

The Index and Tables dialog box appears.

To Create and Compile a Table of Contents Page (continued)

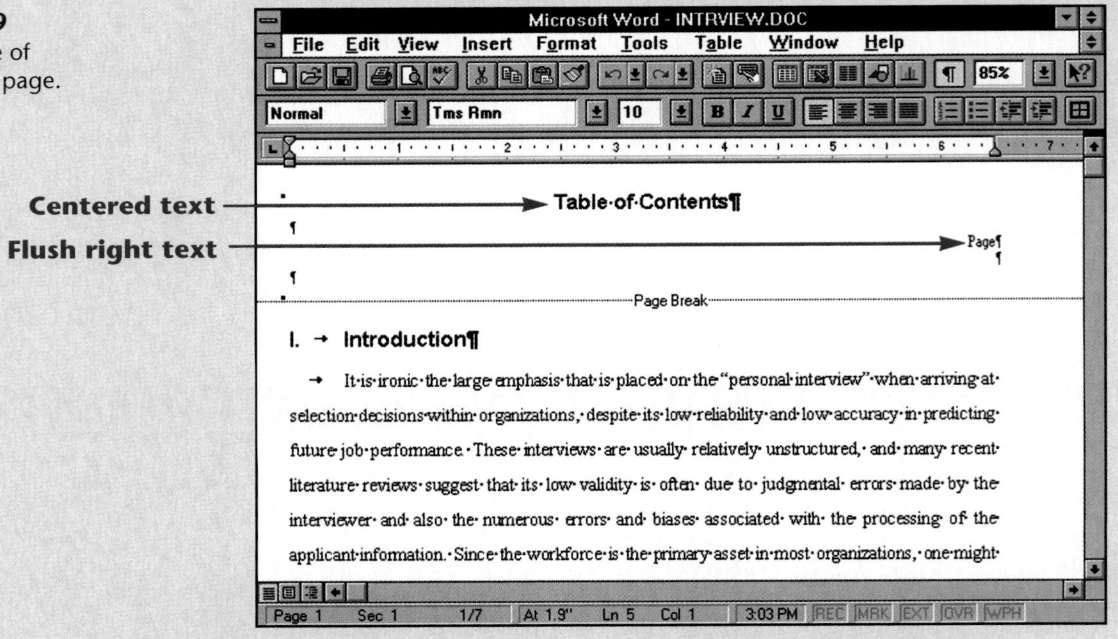

Figure 5.9
The Table of
Contents page.

Centered text ———

Flush right text ———

⑩ Click the Table of Contents tab.

Clicking the Table of Contents tab switches to the Table of Contents page of the Index and Tables dialog box (see Figure 5.10).

Figure 5.10
The Index and Tables
dialog box.

Click here to choose the
Table of Contents style ———►

Sample Table of
Contents ———

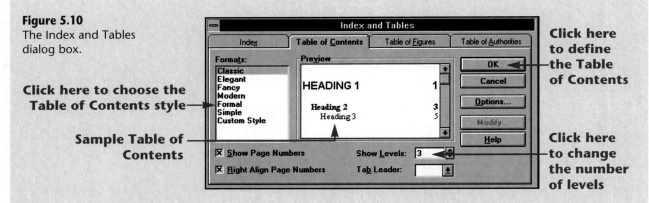

Click here
to define
the Table
of Contents

Click here
to change
the number
of levels

⑪ Choose Formal in the Formats list box.

The Formal style aligns the page numbers flush right, as shown in the Preview area of the dialog box.

⑫ Click the down arrow next to Show Levels one time.

This action changes the number of levels from 3 to 2. The table of contents for this paper only contains the major headings and sub-headings, so you only need two levels.

⑬ Choose OK.

Choosing OK compiles the table of contents. Your table of contents should look similar to Figure 5.11.

Figure 5.11
The completed table of contents for the sample research paper.

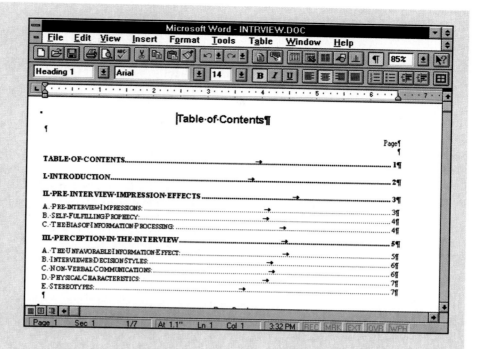

Save your work and keep the INTRVIEW.DOC file open to use in the next lesson, where you learn to create a cross-reference.

You can update a table of contents at any time by selecting the table, and then pressing F9. The Update Table of Contents dialog box appears; you can then choose to update just the page numbers or the entire table. If you add text to the document, you can simply update the page numbers. If you add or delete headings that should appear in the table, however, you need to update the entire table.

Lesson 6: Creating a Cross-Reference

Large documents often contain references to other locations in the document. On page 10 of a document, for example, you may find the reference "see page 15." The problem with such cross-references is that, after you type the reference on page 10, you may add or delete material, moving what was on page 15 to page 16 or 14.

If you try to update a document that has many cross-references manually, you probably won't produce a final document with accurate cross-references. Fortunately, Word can take care of cross-referencing for you. Using the Cross-reference feature, you can create a reference to any item in a document, and then let Word keep track of its location as you edit the document. Try creating a cross-reference in the research paper now.

To Create a Cross-Reference

❶ In the INTRVIEW.DOC file, position the insertion point on the period at the end of the first sentence that ends ...the first five minutes.

You should find the sentence under the heading C. Non-Verbal Communications at the bottom of page five. This sentence refers to a point made earlier in the document that appeared in the section titled The Unfavorable Information Effect.

❷ Insert a space; then type (see the section titled "The Unfavorable Information Effect" on page

Make sure you insert a space after the word page. This space is where you create the cross-reference, which inserts the correct page number for you. Note that you also insert a closing parenthesis later to complete the reference.

❸ Choose Insert, Cross-reference.

The Cross-reference dialog box appears (see Figure 5.12). In the Reference **T**ype list box, Heading is first in the list, so it is already selected. When Heading is selected, all the headings in the report are listed in the For **W**hich Heading list box. This list of headings makes it easy for you to select which heading you want to tie the reference to.

Figure 5.12
Use the Cross-reference dialog box to create cross-references in your document.

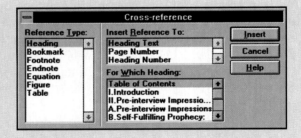

❹ Scroll down through the For Which Heading list box, and select the A. The Unfavorable Infor... **heading.**

This item is an abbreviation for the A. The Unfavorable Information Effect heading, the section to which you refer the reader. A cross-reference is most helpful when you provide a page number so the reader can quickly turn back, review the material, and then continue reading the report.

❺ Choose Page Number in the Insert Reference To list box.

Choosing Page Number tells Word that you want to include the correct page number in the reference text.

⑥ Choose Insert; then choose Close.

The Insert option inserts the page number for the cross-reference (see Figure 5.13). Choosing Close clears the Cross-reference dialog box.

Figure 5.13
The page number of the cross-reference inserted in the text.

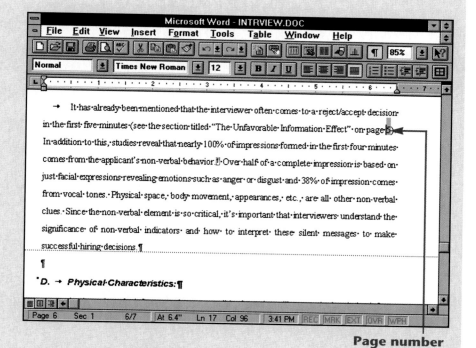

Page number

⑦ Type a close parentheses,); then type a period to end the sentence.

The close parentheses completes the reference phrase you added to this paragraph. You need to display the page number in the reference text.

Save your work and print two copies of INTRVIEW.DOC—one to keep and one to turn in. Close INTRVIEW.DOC after printing. If you have completed your session on the computer, exit Word for Windows and the Windows Program Manager before turning off the computer. Otherwise, continue with the "Applying Your Skills" case studies at the end of this project.

In order to reference headings in a document, you must have given the headings one of Word's heading styles. (You took care of this when you assigned heading styles for the table of contents in the previous lesson.)

If you need to update a cross-reference after you have edited the document, select the reference, and press F9. Word automatically updates all the cross-references when you print the document.

Checking Your Skills

True/False

For each of the following statements, check *T* or *F* to indicate whether the statement is true or false.

__T __F   **1.** You can start a search from anywhere in a document.

__T __F   **2.** Replace **All** stops and ask you to confirm each replacement before it finishes the search.

__T __F   **3.** Endnotes function essentially the same as footnotes, except that they appear on a page by themselves at the beginning of the document.

__T __F   **4.** You have to manually update cross-references in Word.

__T __F   **5.** You can update just the page numbers or the entire table in the Update Table of Contents dialog box.

Multiple Choice

Circle the letter of the correct answer for each of the following.

1. In Word, footnotes are shown in a separate area called the _____.

   a. Note window

   b. Note pane

   c. Footnote/Endnote area

   d. Footnote/Endnote section

2. The Formal style for a table of contents has a _____.

   a. table of contents entry with a page number in parentheses next to the entry

   b. table of contents entry followed by a comma, then the page number

   c. table of contents entry with dot leaders out to the page number, which is flush against the right margin

   d. table of contents entry with the page number on the next line against the left margin

3. The Find feature _____.

   a. searches through your document and counts the number of times a word is used

   b. searches through the document and stops when the word (or word pattern) is found

   c. finds your insertion point for you

   d. searches through the document and tells you what page the word (or word pattern) is on

4. The Index and Tables command appears on the _____ menu.

   a. Format

   b. Tools

   c. Insert

   d. View

5. Word provides _____ Heading styles that you can use on your documents.

   a. thirteen

   b. nine

   c. three

   d. seven

Completion

In the blank provided, write the correct answer for each of the following statements.

1. Use the _____ feature to refer the reader to related pieces of information in a document.

2. The Footnote feature is frequently used to indicate the _____ of outside information in a document.

3. The _____ feature is used to search for a word or word pattern and replace it with another word or word pattern.

4. A heading that will be used in a cross-reference must be assigned one of the _____ styles provided by Word.

5. Footnote text is inserted at the bottom of the page that contains the _____.

Applying Your Skills

Take a few minutes to practice the skills you have learned in this project by completing the "On Your Own" and "Brief Cases" case studies.

On Your Own

Completing the Loan Proposal

Now that you have spent some time working with the features in this project, you can add these elements to the loan proposal you designed for the Rollerblading Club in Project 4.

To Enhance the Loan Proposal

1. Open the file PROJ0502.DOC, and save it as **LOANPRP2.DOC**.

2. Search through the proposal for the loan amount you requested so you can verify that you used the correct figure throughout the proposal.

3. Insert a footnote at the first instance of the club budget figures in order to reference their source, the club's financial statements.

4. Create a cross-reference that refers readers to a page number in the financial statement you would need in this proposal (you can use your own page number).

5. Create a table of contents that lists all the headings in the report.

6. Save your work, and print two copies of the file.

Brief Cases

Completing the Annual Report

Use the skills you have learned in this project to add footnotes, a table of contents, and the appropriate cross-references to the annual report you created for Sound Byte Music in the "Brief Cases" case study for Project 4.

Include a footnote that identifies the financial statements accompanying the report. Use cross-references to refer readers to 1995 figures when 1996 figures are presented with expansion plans and advertising budget. A table of contents should include all headings in the report.

To Add Items to the Annual Report

1. Open the file PROJ0503.DOC, and save it as **ANULRPT2.DOC**.

2. Add a footnote that identifies the financial statement as a source document for the report.

3. Add a cross-reference to the 1995 figures in the discussion about 1996 expansion plans and the proposed advertising campaign.

4. Select the headings, and mark them for entry in the table of contents.

5. Create a Table of Contents page with a title and a page number heading.

6. Define the table of contents on the page you created.

7. Compile the table of contents, and update the cross-reference.

8. Save your work, and print two copies of the file.

Project

6

Using Tables and Graphics

Completing a Newsletter

In this project, you learn how to

- ➤ Create a Table
- ➤ Enter Text into a Table
- ➤ Format a Table
- ➤ Calculate Values in a Table
- ➤ Insert a Picture
- ➤ Move and Resize a Picture

Why Would I Do This?

The Table feature is one of the most versatile and easy-to-use features in Word. Although you can use the Table feature in many ways, people most often use this feature for information that needs to be formatted into columns. You could use the Columns feature to accomplish this task, but the Table feature is easier to use and has more options for formatting the information and the table itself. In fact, the Table AutoFormat tool lets you assign complex formatting with just a few mouse clicks. The Table feature also has several built-in spreadsheet functions that enable you to perform basic mathematical operations.

Pictures can also be added to your documents to illustrate a point, to add excitement, or to add creative flair. You can add pictures that you create in Word, as well as pictures from other programs. Stock graphics called clip art are available through software stores, mail order catalogs, and on-line services. In fact, Word includes a wide variety of clip art that you can use in both formal and informal documents.

You use tables and pictures in this project to put the finishing touches on a newsletter for the members of the Rollerblading Club.

Lesson 1: Creating a Table

Word Tables are very similar to spreadsheet software, such as Excel, both in operation and in terminology. Both spreadsheets and Word Tables are comprised of a grid of columns and rows. When you create a table, you need to estimate how many columns and how many rows (or lines) you will need. Try creating a table in Word now.

To Create a Table

❶ Open the PROJ0601.DOC file, and save it as NEWSLTR.DOC.

The sample newsletter has two columns underneath the title (or masthead). This formatting is accomplished by creating a new section that allows the text to be formatted into columns. Note the *section break* at the top of the newsletter (see Figure 6.1).

❷ Position the insertion point on the blank line above the heading Weekend Roll.

You want to create the table for the officer phone numbers in this spot.

 ❸ Click the Insert Table icon.

Word displays an empty grid. You have to click and drag the mouse to highlight the number of rows and columns you need. Drag the mouse slowly until you get the hang of it.

Figure 6.1
The sample newsletter.

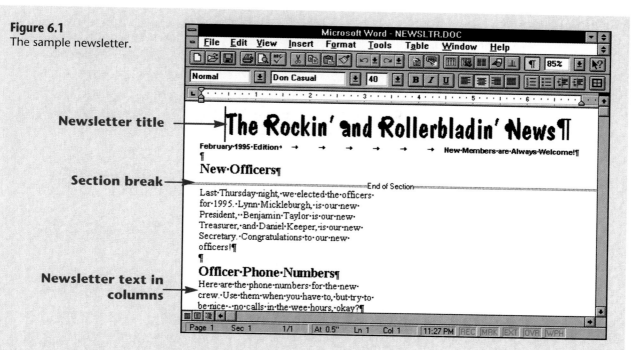

Newsletter title ────→

Section break ────→

Newsletter text in columns ────→

④ **Click and drag the mouse over and down until the bottom of the grid reads** 3x2 Table; **then release the mouse button.**

The number 3 represents the number of rows; the number 2 represents the number of columns. Make sure you have two columns and three rows selected.

If you have problems...

If you have problems clicking and dragging across this grid, you can create the table using the T**a**ble menu. Before you use this method, drag the mouse back through the grid until the bottom reads Cancel. Next, choose T**a**ble, **I**nsert Table. The Insert Table dialog box appears. Use the arrows next to the Number of **C**olumns and Number of **R**ows to specify 2 columns and 3 rows. Choose OK to create the table.

If you have already inserted the table, but you chose the wrong dimensions, use the **U**ndo command to remove the table. Then, try again, either by clicking the **I**nsert Table icon or by choosing **I**nsert Table option from the T**a**ble menu.

Word creates the table at the insertion point. Notice how the table is created within the margins of the newsletter column and that both columns of the table have the same width. By default, Word creates evenly spaced columns between the available margin space. You can easily change the column widths, if necessary. Your newsletter should now look like Figure 6.2.

continues

To Create a Table (continued)

Figure 6.2
The sample newsletter with the table.

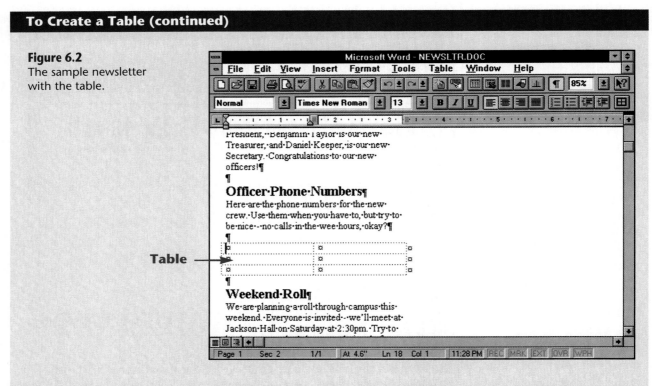

Table

The table includes dotted lines, called *gridlines*, which help you see the *cells* of the table.

Save your work and keep the NEWSLTR.DOC file open to use in the next lesson, where you learn to enter text into a table.

Jargon Watch

Tables are composed of rows and columns. The intersection of a row and a column is called a **cell**. In spreadsheets, **rows** are numbered from top to bottom and **columns** are labeled with letters from left to right. In addition, each cell has a unique address, called a **cell address**. A cell address is composed of the column letter, followed by the row number. For example, the top left cell is A1.

Gridlines, dotted lines in and around the table, help you see the size and position of the table cells. These lines don't normally print, unless you convert some or all of the gridlines to printable lines. A **section break** divides a document into different sections, which you can format separately.

Lesson 2: Entering Text into a Table

Typing text into a table works the same as typing text into the document window, with only a few differences. One difference is that you use the Tab⇄ and ⇧Shift+Tab⇄ keys to move between the cells of a table. Tab⇄

moves you one cell to the right; ⬆Shift+Tab moves you one cell to the left. When you type information into a cell, the text wraps within the margins of the cell so that you don't have to worry about the size of the cell.

In the newsletter document, you need to type each officer's name in the first column and the officer's phone number in the second column. Try entering text into the table now.

The insertion point already appears in the first cell (Word puts it there when you create the table), so you can start typing the first entry.

To Enter Text Into a Table

1 In the NEWSLTR.DOC file, type Rebecca Smith-Bailey.

You enter the new president's name first, followed by her phone number.

2 Press Tab.

Pressing Tab moves you one cell to the right. You type Rebecca's phone number here.

3 Type 581-3731.

Unless you change the alignment, Word aligns the text against the left side of the cell. You can also center text or align text flush right in the cell.

4 Press Tab.

When you press Tab in the last cell of a row, your insertion point moves to the first cell in the next row.

5 Type Benjamin Taylor; then press Tab.

The new treasurer's name appears in the second row.

6 Type 581-4415, then press Tab.

Your insertion point should now be positioned in the first cell of the last row.

7 Type Daniel Keeper; then press Tab.

The new secretary's name appears in the last row.

8 Type 581-1150.

Don't press Tab again—if you do, Word automatically creates a new row that you don't need. Your table should now look like Figure 6.3.

Save your work and keep the NEWSLTR.DOC file open to use in the next lesson, where you learn to format a table.

continues

To Enter Text into a Table (continued)

Figure 6.3
The completed table with names and phone numbers.

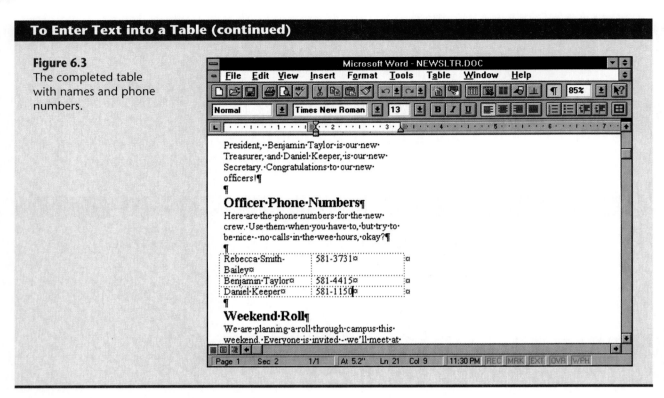

 You can also use the mouse to position the insertion point inside a table. To move the insertion point to a specific cell, position the mouse pointer on the cell, and click the left mouse button.

Lesson 3: Formatting a Table

When you create a new table, Word uses a number of default format settings. As mentioned, gridlines appear inside the table and form the outside border; the text is aligned against the left side of the cell, and the columns have equal widths. Word's Table AutoFormat feature enables you to adjust the format of your table using preset templates.

You can also adjust individual format settings such as column width. Try formatting the newsletter table now.

To Format a Table

❶ In the NEWSLTR.DOC file, position the mouse pointer on the *vertical gridline* between the first and second columns.

When you position the mouse pointer on this gridline, the mouse pointer changes to a double vertical line with arrows on either side (see Figure 6.4). You use this *sizing pointer* to adjust the width of the columns.

Figure 6.4
The mouse pointer adjusts the column widths in the table.

Sizing pointer

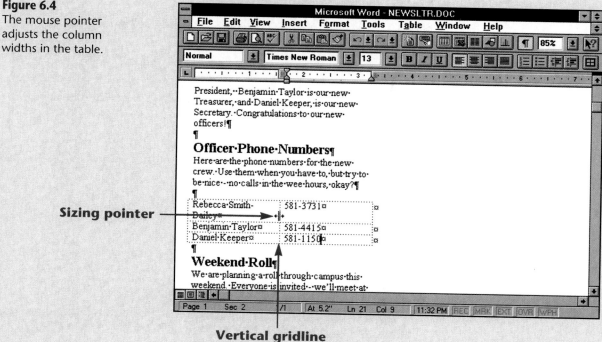

Vertical gridline

2 Click and drag the gridline to the right.

When you click the vertical gridline with the sizing pointer, a dotted guide line, running from the ruler down to the status line, appears. As you drag the mouse, this line helps you see the new column width. You need to increase the size of the left column so that the officers' full names fit on one line (about a quarter of an inch).

3 Release the mouse button.

Releasing the mouse button clears the guideline and adjusts the width of the columns. Your table should now look like Figure 6.5.

If you have problems...

If the name (Rebecca Smith-Bailey) still won't fit on one line in the table, click and drag the vertical gridline farther to the right. Make sure you wait until the sizing pointer appears before you click and drag the gridline.

continues

To Format a Table (continued)

Figure 6.5
Resizing the left column allows more room for the officer names.

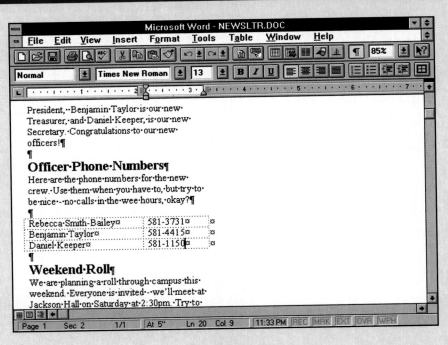

4 Position the insertion point inside the first cell of the table.

5 Choose Table; then choose Table AutoFormat.

The Table AutoFormat dialog box appears (see Figure 6.6). A list of available styles appears down the left side of the dialog box. When you choose a style, the sample table changes to reflect the formatting options for that style.

Figure 6.6
The Table AutoFormat dialog box.

Select a style from this list

Use this scroll bar to move through the list

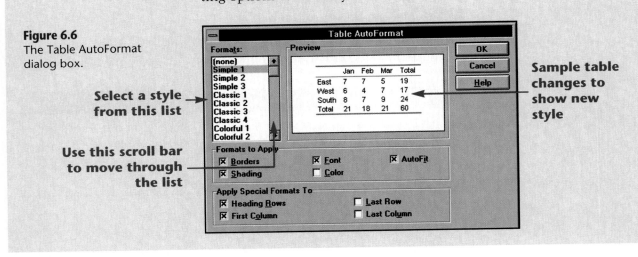

Sample table changes to show new style

⑥ Press the ⬇ several times.

Take a minute and scroll through the list so you can see the variety of styles available.

⑦ Select Grid 1 in the list of Formats; then choose OK.

The Grid 1 style is applied to the table, which should look like Figure 6.7. The table has a single line border and single grid lines within the table.

Figure 6.7
The table with the
Grid 1 style.

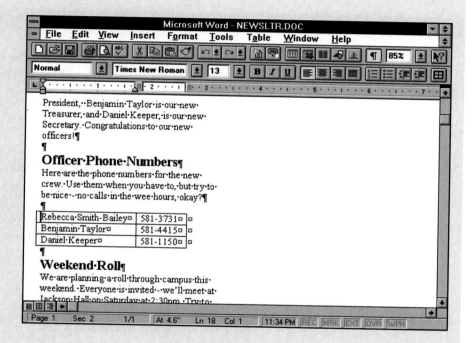

Save your work and keep the NEWSLTR.DOC file open to use in the next lesson, where you learn to perform calculations using a table.

Jargon Watch

A **vertical gridline** separates two columns in a table. A **sizing pointer** appears when the mouse passes over a vertical gridline. When this pointer appears, you can click and drag the gridline to resize column widths in a table.

You can use the Cell Height and Width dialog box to format rows and columns in a table. Choose T**a**ble; then choose Cell Height and **W**idth to open the dialog box. The **R**ow page has options to align text to the left, center, or right of a cell. You can also set a specific row height on the **R**ow page. Click the **C**olumn tab to switch to the **C**olumns page, which lets you move across the columns in a table and specify a particular width (in inches) for each. This page has an **A**utoFit option that automatically adjusts the width of the column to accommodate the contents.

Lesson 4: Calculating Values in a Table

Value
A numeric cell entry.

Word's Table feature includes several built-in spreadsheet functions that you can use to perform mathematical calculations. The most common calculation, the Sum formula, adds *values* together to produce a total.

The table at the bottom of the newsletter shows expenses for the Rollerblading Club's trip to Colorado. The first column lists the expense items for the trip; the second column will show the dollar amount for each item. Try entering values and calculating a total in the table now.

To Calculate Values In a Table

❶ **In the NEWSLTR.DOC file, position the insertion point in the second row of the second column in the expense table.**

Note that the insertion point should align against the right side of the cell (see Figure 6.8). The cells that will contain values have been formatted to align flush right.

Figure 6.8
In this table, the values will align flush right.

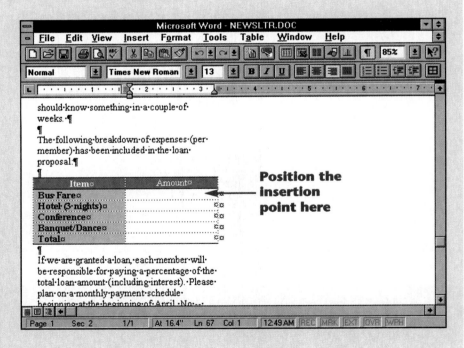

❷ **Type 125.00; then press ↓.**

The expense for the bus fare is $125.00. Pressing ↓ moves you to the next row in the column.

❸ **Type 75.50; then press ↓.**

The expense for the hotel room is $75.50. Notice how the numbers align by decimal points.

❹ **Type 100.00; then press ↓.**

The expense for conference registration is $100.00.

⑤ Type 35.00; then press ↓.

The expense for the conference banquet and dance is $35.00. Your table should now look like Figure 6.9.

Figure 6.9
The table with the values entered.

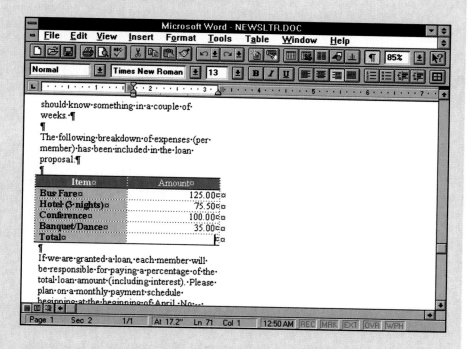

The insertion point should appear in the last cell in the second column. Because you want the total amount to appear in this column, you insert a formula to calculate that amount here.

⑥ Choose Table, Formula.

The Formula dialog box appears with the suggested formula (see Figure 6.10). Word presumes that you want to add the numbers in the column and place the total inside this cell. Next, choose a format for the total amount.

Figure 6.10
The Formula dialog box with the suggested formula.

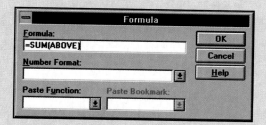

⑦ Choose Number Format.

Choosing **N**umber Format opens a drop-down list of formats for the result of the calculation.

continues

To Calculate Values in a Table (continued)

8 **Choose the third format in the list — $#,##0.00;($#,##0.00).**

This format places a dollar sign at the beginning of the total amount, inserts a comma if you have a number greater than 999.99, and uses two decimal places.

9 **Choose OK.**

Choosing OK inserts the result of the SUM formula in the cell, using the chosen format. The table should now look like Figure 6.11.

Figure 6.11
The expense table with the total amount calculated.

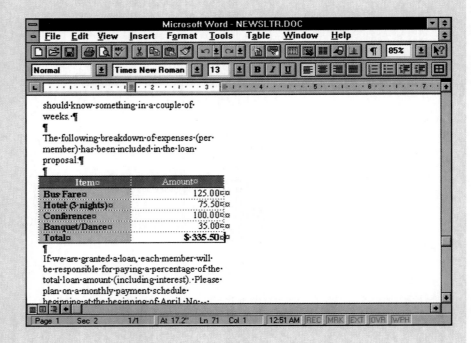

Save your work and keep the NEWSLTR.DOC file open to use in the next lesson, where you learn to insert a picture.

If you change any of the values in cells that are included in a formula or if you alter a formula, you need to recalculate the table. Select the cell containing the total amount; then press F9 to update the amount.

Lesson 5: Inserting a Picture

Word makes it easy for you to insert pictures in your documents, either by creating your own pictures, or by importing graphics files from other programs. Word accepts most popular graphic file formats, including Windows bitmap files (BMP) and metafiles (WMF). The clip art images that come with Word are yet another source of artwork. Try inserting a picture into the newsletter now.

To Insert a Picture

❶ In the NEWSLTR.DOC file, position the insertion point at the beginning of the paragraph under the heading Boulder or Bust!

You want to insert the picture at this spot in the document.

❷ Choose Insert, Picture.

The Insert Picture dialog box appears (see Figure 6.12). In most cases, the Word 6.0 for Windows Clip Art directory automatically displays. If that directory doesn't appear in your dialog box, use the drive and directory lists to locate this directory. Word includes over 90 graphic files that you can use in your documents.

Figure 6.12
Use the Insert Picture dialog box to choose a clip art file.

Use this scroll bar to view the clip art files

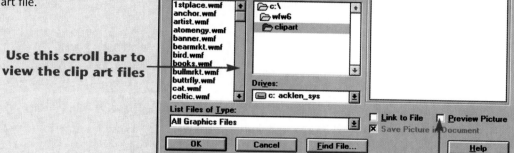

Click here to preview the picture

❸ Select the WINTER.WMF file in the File Name list box.

You insert this picture into the document. If you can't find WINTER.WMF, use another picture that you deem appropriate.

❹ Choose OK.

Word inserts the picture in its original size at the insertion point (see Figure 6.13).

Save your work and keep the NEWSLTR.DOC file open to use in the next lesson, where you learn to move and resize a picture.

continues

To Insert a Picture (continued)

Figure 6.13
The WINTER.WMF file inserted into the paragraph.

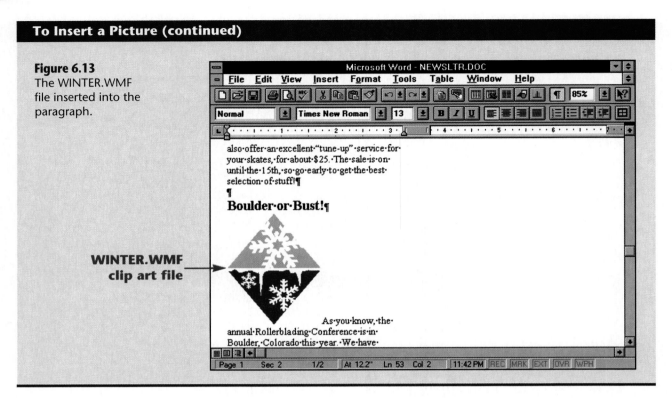

WINTER.WMF clip art file

You can preview a graphics file by selecting the **P**review Picture option in the Insert Picture dialog box. As you select each file, you can preview the clip art files available in Word.

Lesson 6: Moving and Resizing a Picture

When you insert a picture into a document, Word maintains the original size of the graphic image. You can easily resize the picture to suit your needs.

The easiest way to move and resize a picture is with the mouse. When you select a picture, sizing handles appear on all four sides. The location of the sizing handles indicates which way the box will be resized. If you click and drag a sizing handle on the corner, you can resize the box in two directions at once. Moving a picture is easy—you just click and drag the picture to the new position.

In the Rollerblading Club newsletter, you need to size the graphic box so it takes up roughly one-half the column width. You also need to move the box into the paragraph so the first two to three lines of the text are above the picture and the rest of the lines wrap around it. Try moving and resizing the image now.

To Move and Resize a Picture

❶ In the NEWSLTR.DOC file, click the picture.

Clicking the picture selects it. When you select a picture, a border with eight small squares appears around the picture (see Figure 6.14). The squares—called *sizing handles*—let you increase and decrease the size of a picture.

Figure 6.14
A border and sizing handles appear around a selected picture.

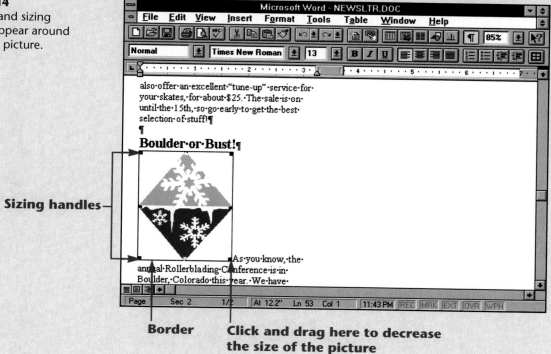

Sizing handles—

Border   Click and drag here to decrease the size of the picture

❷ Position the mouse pointer over the sizing handle at the lower right corner of the picture.

The mouse pointer should change to a two-sided diagonal arrow.

❸ Click and drag the sizing handle upward and to the left. Resize the picture until it becomes roughly one half the width of the column.

When you drag a sizing handle, a dotted guide line appears to show you how big the box will become when you release the mouse button (see Figure 6.15).

continues

To Move or Resize a Picture (continued)

Figure 6.15
The dotted line acts as a guide while you resize the box.

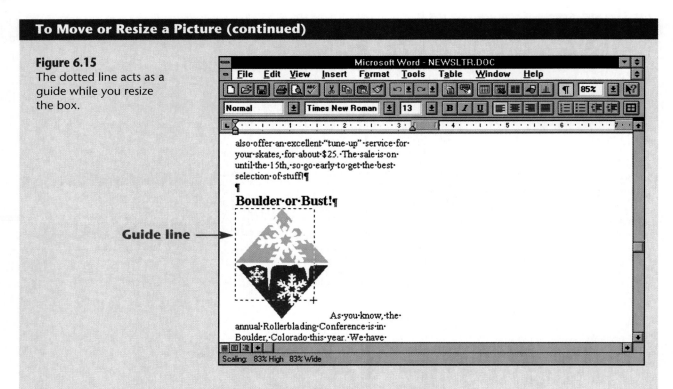

Guide line

❹ Release the mouse button.

When you release the mouse button, Word resizes the picture to fit the new dimensions. Now, you need to move the picture down into the paragraph. In order to do this, you have to place a frame around the picture because a framed picture allows the text to wrap around it. Do this now. If the picture is not still selected, click the picture now to select it before you continue.

❺ Choose Insert, Frame.

Word displays a message indicating that you tried to insert a frame while in Normal view. The message also states that you have to switch to the *Page Layout view* to see, resize, or reposition the frame.

❻ Choose Yes.

When you choose Yes, Word switches you to Page Layout view mode, which allows you to see all the page elements on-screen. Notice how the columns display side-by-side in this view. A frame appears around the picture (see Figure 6.16). The mouse pointer changes to a pointer with a four-sided arrow attached to it.

Figure 6.16
The picture now has a frame.

Click and drag the framed picture down into the paragraph

Edge of the paper

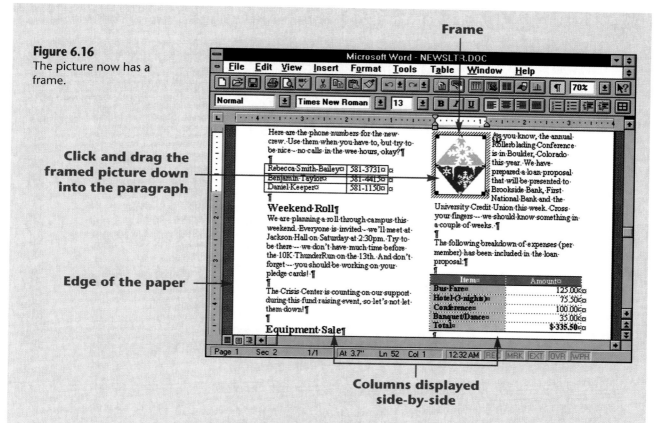

Frame

Columns displayed side-by-side

❼ Click and drag the framed picture down into the paragraph.

You want to drag the picture down into the paragraph so the first three lines appear above the picture; the bottom of the picture should line up with the last line in the paragraph. You may have to make small adjustments to move the picture to this position. When you finish, your newsletter should look similar to the one shown in Figure 6.17.

continues

To Move or Resize a Picture (continued)

Figure 6.17
The text of the paragraph wraps around the graphic box.

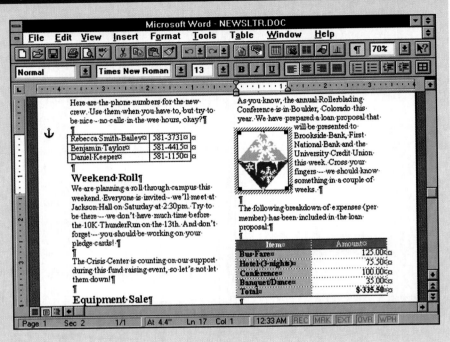

❽ Click inside the document window.

Clicking inside the document window deselects the picture. You have now completed the newsletter.

Save your work and print two copies of NEWSLTR.DOC, one to keep and one to turn in. Close NEWSLTR.DOC after printing. If you have completed your session on the computer, exit Word for Windows and the Windows Program Manager before turning off the computer. Otherwise, continue with the "Applying Your Skills" case studies at the end of this project.

Jargon Watch

Sizing handles are small squares on a picture border that you use to size a picture. A corner sizing handle sizes in two directions at the same time. The **Page Layout view** shows you all of the elements of a page. When you work with certain features of the program, you receive prompting to switch to the Page Layout view.

You can actually edit a picture in Word. Just double-click the picture to open a new window for the picture. Word displays the Drawing toolbar inside the document window. You can use the icons on this toolbar to create and edit pictures.

Checking Your Skills

True/False

For each of the following statements, check *T* or *F* to indicate whether the statement is true or false.

__T __F **1.** The Table AutoFormat feature has a series of styles that you can choose from to format a table.

__T __F **2.** Tables can be used to format text and numbers into columns.

__T __F **3.** The spreadsheet functions in Word are similar to those seen in powerful spreadsheet programs.

__T __F **4.** Pictures are used to insert graphic images into a document.

__T __F **5.** A table formula is inserted as a field.

Multiple Choice

Circle the letter of the correct answer for each of the following.

1. You can place _____ in a document.

    a. Windows bit maps

    b. Windows metafiles

    c. Word clip art files

    d. all of the above

2. The most commonly-used calculation in the Table feature is _____.

    a. Average

    b. Minimum Value

    c. Maximum Value

    d. Sum

3. You must insert a _____ around a picture to allow text to wrap around the picture.

    a. border

    b. frame

    c. sizing handles

    d. style

4. In a table, pressing ⇧Shift+Tab⇆ moves you _____.

    a. one cell to the right

    b. one cell to the left

    c. to the top cell of a table

    d. to the bottom cell of a table

5. The Word clip art files have the _____ extension.

    a. PCX

    b. WMF

    c. WPG

    d. EPS

Completion

In the blank provided, write the correct answer for each of the following statements.

1. A _____ formula adds a series of numbers together.

2. Word includes over _____ graphic files that you can use in your documents.

3. A table _____ is the intersection of a row and a column.

4. The cell address is composed of the column _____ and the row _____.

5. You can resize a picture with sizing _____.

Applying Your Skills

Take a few minutes to practice the skills you have learned in this project by completing the "On Your Own" and "Brief Cases" case studies.

On Your Own

Create a Party Invitation

Now that you have spent some time working with Word's Tables feature and picture capability, you can create an invitation for a card party you plan next weekend for the Rollerblading Club. Club members will provide the following food and drinks: pizza, salad, bread sticks, brownies, cookies, and soft drinks. Use a table to list the members who are bringing food and drinks, along with the menu items each person will provide. Insert a picture from the Word clip art to liven up the invitation.

To Create the Invitation

1. Open a new document, and then create a heading using one of the decorative fonts included in Word.

2. Type a greeting; then list the items you will serve at the party. Use a different font for this text.

3. Type a short paragraph introducing the table that lists the guests and the food items they have agreed to bring. Ask guests to bring additional decks of cards for card games.

4. Create a table with the names of the members and the food items they have agreed to bring.

5. Choose a picture from the Word clip art, and insert it into the invitation.

6. Resize and move the picture to position it within the invitation text.

7. Save the invitation as **CLUBINV.DOC**, and then print two copies of it.

Brief Cases

Create a Company Newsletter

Use the skills you have learned in this project to create a company newsletter for the employees of Sound Byte Music. Include information about new releases, new employees, and plans for a company picnic. Create a table listing the top ten sellers for the previous month. Create another table listing new employees and their telephone numbers. Insert at least one picture to "spice up" the newsletter.

To Create the Newsletter

1. Open a new document, and then create a heading using one of the decorative fonts included in Word.

2. Use a smaller font size to enter the date of the newsletter and the company name. Position the company name flush left and the date flush right.

3. Start with information on new releases. In this section, type a short introductory paragraph for the Top Ten table.

4. Create a table for the Top Ten Sellers of last month. Create columns for (1) This week's number, (2) Title, and (3) Last month's position on the chart.

5. Type in the ten best selling albums/cassettes/CDs.

6. Use the Table AutoFormat feature to format the Top Ten table. Choose an informal, flashy style.

7. Type a paragraph or two describing plans for the company picnic next weekend. Give the time and location.

8. Type a short paragraph introducing three new employees.

9. Create a table for the names of new employees and their phone numbers.

10. Choose a Word clip art image and insert it into the document. Size and position the image in the newsletter.

11. Save the file as **COMPNEWS.DOC**, and then print two copies of it.

Project 7

7

Using Merge

Setting up a Mail Merge

In this project, you learn how to

➤ Identify the Main Document

➤ Create the Data Source

➤ Enter Information into the Data Source

➤ Create the Main Document

➤ Create an Envelope Main Document

➤ Merge the Files

Why Would I Do This?

When you want to send a personalized letter to a number of people, you can use Word's Merge feature. Consider the cover letter that you created in Project 2. If you need to send your resume out to a number of people, you can save time by setting up the cover letter as a form file and then merging in the names and addresses of the recipients. The result, a personalized letter, gives the impression that you typed each letter individually. In reality, you only typed the letter once.

For this project, you send out a notice to all the members of the Rollerblading Club. Using the notice as your sample document and the instructions provided in this project, you learn how to use the Merge feature to create a notice and an envelope for each club member.

Lesson 1: Identifying the Main Document

A merge has two types of files: a *main document* and a *data source*. The main document contains the information that stays the same for all the recipients—in this case, the notice. In the areas where you need to insert information from the data source, you insert *merge fields* into the main document that match the merge fields you used in the data source. When you merge the two documents together, Word matches up the merge fields and inserts the information into the appropriate spot.

You can either create a main document from an existing document, or you can start from scratch. In this case, the notice you plan to send has already been created, so you need to identify the notice as the main document.

To Identify the Main Document

❶ Open the PROJ0701.DOC file, and save it as CLUBMTG.DOC.

CLUBMTG.DOC is the notice you want to send out to the club members.

❷ Choose Tools, Mail Merge.

The Mail Merge Helper dialog box appears (see Figure 7.1). The Mail Merge Helper provides you with steps for creating both the main documents and the data source, and then merging the files together.

continues

To Identify the Main Document (continued)

Figure 7.1
Use the Mail Merge
Helper dialog box to
create main document
and data source files.

Instruction message

Click here to
create the main
document

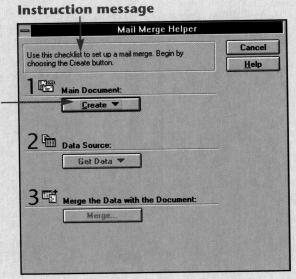

❸ **Choose Create.**

Choosing **C**reate opens a drop-down list of the different main documents you can create with the Mail Merge Helper.

❹ **Choose Form Letters.**

Word displays a message box asking if you want to use the CLUBMTG.DOC document in the Active Window or in a new document window (start from scratch).

❺ **Choose Active Window.**

The Mail Merge Helper dialog box reappears with a message below the Main Document section, indicating a merge type of Form Letters. The name and location of the main document appear in the dialog box (see Figure 7.2).

Figure 7.2
The Mail Merge Helper
dialog box after a main
document has been
identified.

Type of merge

Name and location
of main document

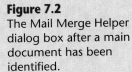
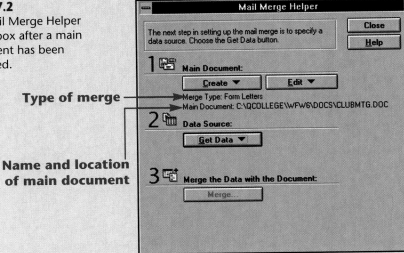

You complete the next step, creating the data source, in the next lesson. Make sure you leave the Mail Merge Helper dialog box open so that you can use it in the next lesson.

In Word, you have two files in a merge—the data source and the main document. The **data source** contains the information that is inserted into the main document (names, addresses). The **main document** contains the information that doesn't change from one person to the next (letter, notice, invitation). When you create the main document, you place **merge fields,** markers that indicate where you want to insert information from the data source, inside the document. These merge fields must match up to the merge fields used in the data source.

In the data source, each piece of information is called a field. You can have an unlimited number of fields. A **record** is a collection of all the fields for an individual person or item. You can have as many records in the data source as you need. The first record in the data source is called the **header row.** The header row contains a list of the merge fields used in the data source.

Lesson 2: Creating the Data Source

The data source contains the information you need to insert in the main document—in this case, the name and address information. The first step in creating the data source is defining how you want to organize the information. For this lesson, you separate the information into first name and last name fields to give you more flexibility when using the data.

Follow the steps below to define a data source for the members of the Rollerblading club.

To Create the Data Source

❶ In the Mail Merge Helper dialog box, choose Get Data.

Choosing **G**et Data opens a drop-down list of options (see Figure 7.3). You can create a data source from scratch, or you can identify an existing document as a data source. In this lesson, you create the data source from scratch.

continues

To Create the Data Source (continued)

Figure 7.3
You can create a data source from scratch or identify an existing file as the data source.

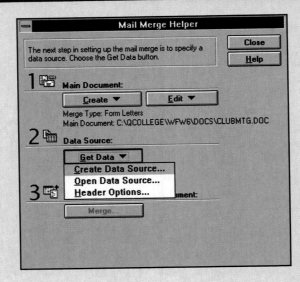

2 Choose Create Data Source.

The Create Data Source dialog box appears, as shown in Figure 7.4. Every data source has a *header row* that lists the merge fields used in the file. The first step to creating a data source is identifying the merge fields for the header row. The Create Data Source dialog box has a predefined list of merge fields that you can use. For this example, you remove the merge fields you don't need.

Figure 7.4
Use the Create Data Source dialog box to specify the merge fields you want to use in the data source file.

Type a new field name here

Click here to add a new field name

Select a field name

Click here to move a field name up in the list

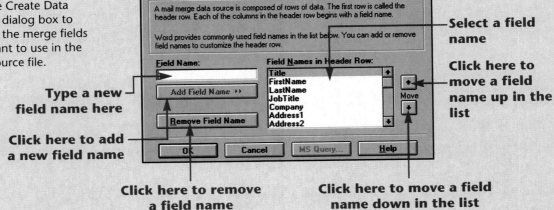

Click here to remove a field name

Click here to move a field name down in the list

3 Click Title in the Field Names in Header Row list box.

Clicking a field name (merge field) selects that field name so that you can remove it, or move it around in the list.

4 **Choose Remove Field Name.**

The **R**emove Field Name option takes the selected field name out of the list. The FirstName field becomes the first field name in the list. You can now remove the JobTitle and Company field names (merge fields) as well.

5 **Click JobTitle in the Field Names in Header Row list box, and choose Remove Field Name.**

You removed the JobTitle field name because the club members are all university students.

6 **Click Company; then choose Remove Field Name.**

Because the club members are all students, you don't need the Company field name either. Word offers two address fields that you can use for multi-line addresses—Address1 and Address2. Each address field holds only one line of information. You need to use both of these fields as well as the City, State, and PostalCode fields; however, you can remove the rest of the fields. Scroll down through the list of merge fields until you can see the Country and phone number (HomePhone and WorkPhone) fields.

7 **Click Country; then choose Remove Field Name.**

Delete the Country field because everyone lives in the United States.

8 **Click HomePhone; then choose Remove Field Name.**

You won't need to enter the member's phone numbers for this mail merge, so go ahead and remove both of the phone number fields.

9 **Click WorkPhone; then choose Remove Field Name.**

The field names (merge fields) in the list box should now match the ones shown in Figure 7.5.

Figure 7.5
The Create Data Source dialog box with all the field names (merge fields).

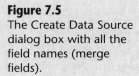

Click here when you finish

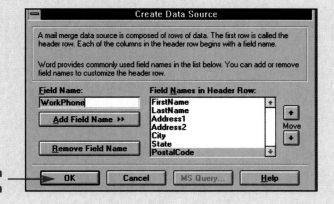

continues

To Create the Data Source (continued)

If you have problems...

If your fields don't appear in the right order, or if you accidentally removed a field, you need to take care of this now. If you need to reinsert a field name, do it now. Type the name of the field in the **F**ield Name text box and choose **A**dd Field Name. Select the new field name; then use the Move arrows to insert it into the correct place in the list. Continue selecting field names (merge fields) and moving them around until they appear in the correct order.

10 Choose OK.

When you choose OK, the Save Data Source dialog box opens (See Figure 7.6). You need to type a file name for the data source here.

Figure 7.6
Type the name of the data source file in the Save Data Source dialog box.

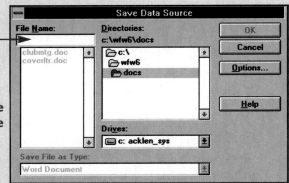

Type the name of the data source file here

11 Type clublist.doc in the File Name text box, and choose OK.

Word saves the data source file, and then displays a message box telling you that you can add records to the data source or insert merge fields into the main document. Keep this message box open to use in Lesson 3, where you enter the name and address information for the Rollerblading Club members.

Part of this lesson involved removing the extra merge fields that you wouldn't use for the Rollerblading Club members. This step is optional because you don't have to type any information in those fields. Entering the name and address information is easier, however, if you only have to work with the fields you use.

Lesson 3: Entering Information into the Data Source

One benefit to creating the data source file using the Rollerblading Club members information is that you can use the file the next time you need to send something to club members. The effort you make now will save you time later.

In this lesson, you type the name and address information into the fields you defined. You should still have the message box displayed on your screen. Try entering the name and address information now.

To Enter Information into the Data Source

❶ Choose Edit Data Source in the message box of the Mail Merge Helper dialog box.

Choosing Edit **D**ata Source opens the Data Form dialog box, where you can enter the name and address information for the Rollerblading Club members (see Figure 7.7).

Figure 7.7
The Data Form dialog box with all the merge fields.

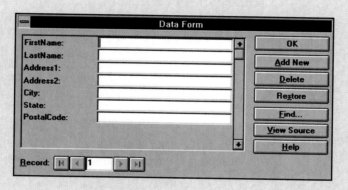

❷ Type Heather in the FirstName text box, and press ⏎Enter.

The Data Form dialog box lets you quickly enter the name and address information in your data source. Pressing ⏎Enter after typing in a field moves you to the next text box where you can type in the next field's information.

❸ Type West in the LastName text box, and press ⏎Enter.

Because you have broken the name into FirstName and LastName fields, you only need the last name here.

❹ Type 1603 Laurel in the Address1 text box, and press ⏎Enter twice.

Because the address only fills one line, you need to press ⏎Enter one extra time to move past the Address2 text box.

❺ Type Edford in the City text box, and press ⏎Enter.

Enter only the name of the city here. Word has separate fields for the city, state, and zip code information.

continues

To Enter Information in the Data Source (continued)

6 **Type Indiana in the State text box, and press** `Enter`.

In the next text box, Word uses the PostalCode field name for the zip code information because other countries call this information a postal code, not a zip code.

7 **Type 46033 in the PostalCode text box.**

Before you press `Enter` in the last field, check the information you have typed, and make sure the information looks correct. Your information in the Data Form dialog box should match Figure 7.8.

Figure 7.8
The Data Form dialog box with the first record entered.

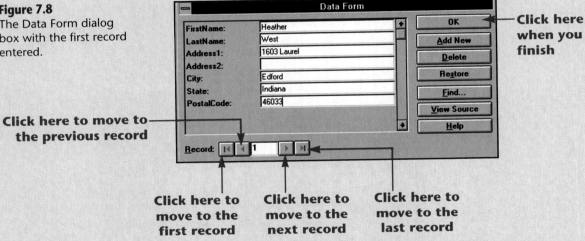

Click here to move to the previous record

Click here when you finish

Click here to move to the first record

Click here to move to the next record

Click here to move to the last record

If you have problems...

If you need to fix mistakes in any of the fields, press `Tab` to move down a field name and `Shift`+`Tab` to move up a field name. You can also click inside the text box in which you need to make the correction.

8 **Press** `Enter`.

Pressing `Enter` in the last field takes you to a new blank record.

9 **Using the preceding steps, enter the following names in the Data Form dialog box:**

Jeffery Andrews
1105-B Jimmy Drive
Bloomington, Indiana 46032

Benjamin Taylor
4801 Allen Street
Apt. 603
Nashville, Indiana 46037

Lynn Mickleburgh
432 Greenlee
Apt. 1601
Martinsville, Indiana 46030

Daniel Keeper
Jackson Hall
2nd Floor South
Bloomington, Indiana
46032

Chuck Sharon
708 West Gibson
Greenwood, Indiana 46293

Patty Clark
8405 Jelson Blvd.
Edford, Indiana 46055

🔟 **Choose View Source.**

Choosing **V**iew Source closes the Data Form dialog box and displays the data source information in the document window, along with a new toolbar—the Database toolbar. The Database toolbar has icons for common tasks you perform when working with merge files.

Notice that Word places the data source information in a table (see Figure 7.9). Don't worry about the way the text wraps inside the table cells—it won't affect the way the text appears when you merge. If you prefer, you can adjust the column widths and format the table, but you don't have to go to the trouble.

Click here to return to the Data Form dialog box

Click here to switch to the main document

Figure 7.9
The data source table with the name and address information filled in.

Database toolbar

Click here to add a new record

Click here to delete a new record

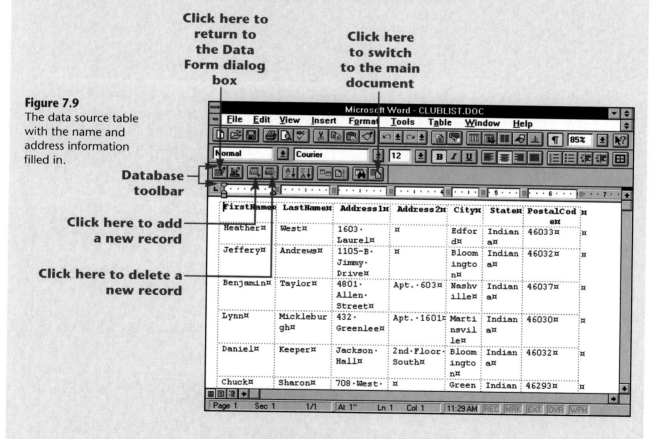

Save your work and keep the CLUBLIST.DOC file open to use in the next lesson, where you learn to create the main document.

Lesson 4: Creating the Main Document

In Lesson 1, you identified the CLUBMTG.DOC file as the file you will use to create the main document file. You have only taken the first step in creating the main document, however. The second step is to insert the merge fields where you want the information from the data source to appear. Try inserting merge fields in the main document file now.

To Create the Main Document

1 In the CLUBLIST.DOC file, click the Mail Merge Main Document icon on the Database toolbar.

Clicking the Mail Merge Main Document icon switches to the main document file, the CLUBMTG.DOC file (see Figure 7.10). Notice that the Mail Merge toolbar appears.

Click here to insert a merge field

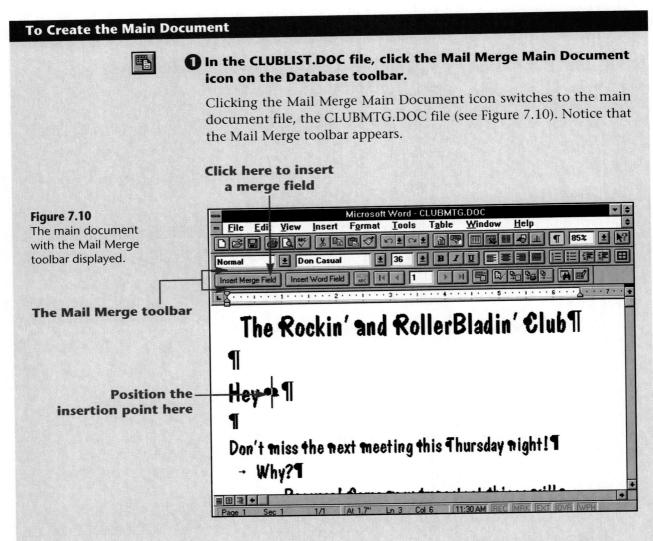

Figure 7.10
The main document with the Mail Merge toolbar displayed.

The Mail Merge toolbar

Position the insertion point here

Because this letter has an informal style, the greeting after the heading reads Hey-. This greeting is the only piece of information from the data source that you use in this main document. The rest of the information goes in the envelope main document.

❷ Position the insertion point between Hey and the dash after the word.

You need to insert the merge field for the first name here. When you merge the main document and the data source, the first name gets inserted here so that each notice is individually addressed.

❸ Click the Insert Merge Field button on the Mail Merge toolbar.

The Insert Merge Field drop-down list appears below the button.

❹ Choose FirstName.

Choosing FirstName inserts the merge field in the main document (see Figure 7.11).

Figure 7.11
The main document with the FirstName merge field.

FirstName merge field

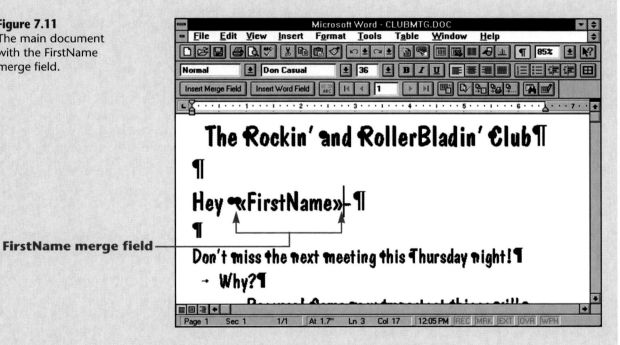

If you have problems...

If you have the Field Codes option selected in the View page of the Options dialog box, your field displays like this: {MERGEFIELD FirstName}.

❺ Double-click the document Control-menu box.

Double-clicking the document Control-menu box closes the document. Choose **Yes**, if you are prompted to save your work.

When this document closes, the CLUBLIST.DOC document should appear. Keep the CLUBLIST.DOC file open to use in the next lesson, where you learn to create envelope mailing addresses.

Lesson 5: Creating an Envelope Main Document

Because you need to mail these notices out to club members, you need to create an envelope main document that you can merge with the data source. The envelope main document contains merge fields for the members' names and addresses.

To Create an Envelope Main Document

 ❶ Click the New icon.

Clicking the New icon opens a new document.

❷ Choose Mail Merge from the Tools menu.

The Mail Merge Helper dialog box appears.

❸ Choose Envelopes from the Create drop-down list.

Word displays a message box stating that you can create the envelope main document in the Active Window, or in a new document window.

❹ Choose Active Window.

The Mail Merge Helper dialog box reappears. You now define the data source you want to associate with this main document.

❺ Choose Open Data Source from the Get Data drop-down list.

The Open Data Source dialog box appears. You need to type the name of the data source file here.

❻ Type clublist.doc in the File Name text box, and choose OK.

You can also double-click the CLUBLIST.DOC file in the file list, if you prefer that method. A message box appears stating that Word needs to set up your main document.

❼ Choose Set Up Main Document.

The Envelope Options dialog box appears (see Figure 7.12). The settings in this dialog box represent standard settings for a business envelope.

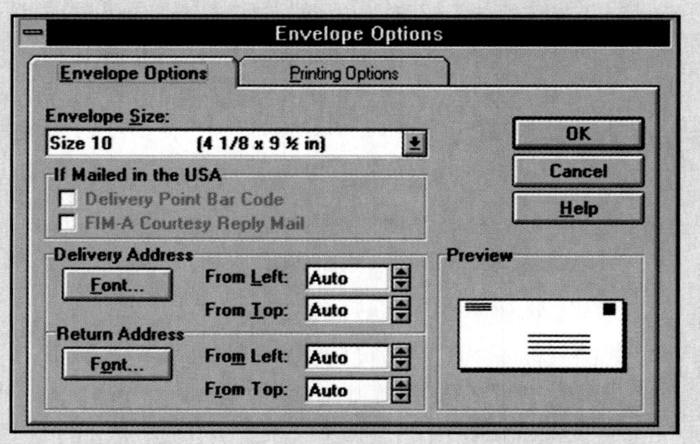

Figure 7.12
Use the Envelope Options dialog box to set the options for the envelope.

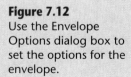

8 Choose OK.

The Envelope Address dialog box appears (see Figure 7.13). You insert the merge fields for the envelope main document at this point.

9 Choose FirstName from the Insert Merge Field drop-down list.

Word inserts the FirstName merge field in the Sample Envelope Address window.

10 Use the Insert Merge Field to insert the merge fields in the following format:

<<FirstName>> <<LastName>>
<<Address1>>
<<Address2>>
<<City>>, <<State>> <<PostalCode>>

When you select the merge field, it inserts the field in brackets as shown below.

Make sure you include the space between the FirstName and LastName, the comma/space between the City and State, and two spaces between the State and PostalCode fields. The Envelope Address dialog box should now look like Figure 7.13.

Figure 7.13
The Envelope Address dialog box with the merge fields in place.

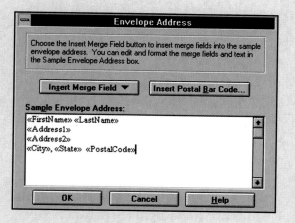

11 Choose OK.

Choosing OK closes the Envelope Address dialog box and returns you to the Mail Merge Helper dialog box. Leave this dialog box open so that you can merge the envelope main document and the data source in the next lesson. You also merge the form letter main document with the data source in the next lesson.

Lesson 6: Merging the Files

Merging the data source and main documents is by far the easiest part of the entire merge process. When you merge the data source and main documents, Word looks through the main document for any merge fields, and then matches these merge fields with the merge fields in the data source.

When a match is found, Word pulls the information from the data source and inserts that information into the main document, replacing the merge fields. A new copy of the main document is created for each record in the data source. Try merging the data source with the main documents now.

To Merge the Files

➊ In the Mail Merge Helper dialog box, choose Merge.

The Merge dialog box appears (see Figure 7.14). The current settings merge all the records in the data source with the envelope main document to create a new document.

Figure 7.14
The Merge dialog box for the envelope main document.

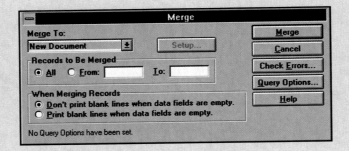

➋ Choose Merge from the Merge dialog box.

When the merge finishes, the first envelope displays (see Figure 7.15). The return address has been pulled from the User Info page of the Options (choose **T**ools, **O**ptions) dialog box. The user information is entered when the program is installed and can be edited from the Options dialog box.

Figure 7.15
The merged envelopes have the name and address information inserted.

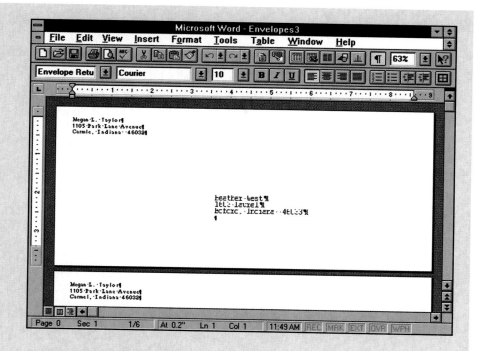

If you have problems...

If a merge doesn't produce the desired results, just close the document that contains the results of the merge. (Don't save the document.) Make the necessary corrections in the data source and main documents; then perform the merge again.

First, make sure you didn't accidentally delete part of the merge field in the main document—the << >> and the field names are very important. If you have deleted any part of the merge field, delete the rest of it; then re-insert the merge field. You can't type this information from the keyboard.

Second, make sure you included the correct spacing and punctuation in the main document. All spacing and punctuation should be included in the main document, not the data source.

Third, make sure the merge fields in both files match exactly. If they don't, Word can't match up the merge fields and insert the information.

 ❸ Click the Print icon.

Clicking the Print icon sends the envelopes to the printer. Most printers accept envelopes through a manual feed tray, so you have to insert the envelopes into the printer. If you don't have envelopes handy, use regular paper.

continues

To Merge the Files (continued)

④ Double-click the document Control-menu box.

Double-clicking the document Control-menu box closes the document window. Word prompts you to save your changes.

⑤ Choose No.

In most cases, you don't need to save the results of a merge because you can always merge the two files together again. When you close the merged envelopes, the envelope main document should appear.

⑥ Click the Save icon.

Clicking the Save icon opens the Save As dialog box.

⑦ Type clubenv.doc in the File Name text box, and choose OK.

Now, open the notice main document (CLUBMTG.DOC) and merge it with the CLUBLIST.DOC data source file.

⑧ Open the CLUBMTG.DOC file.

You created this notice main document file earlier.

 ⑨ Click the Mail Merge Helper icon on the Mail Merge toolbar.

The Mail Merge Helper dialog box appears.

⑩ Choose Merge from the Mail Merge Helper dialog box.

The Merge dialog box appears. The current settings merge all the records in the data source with the envelope main document to a new document.

⑪ Choose Merge.

When the merge finishes, the insertion point appears at the top of the first notice (see Figure 7.16). The member's first name has been inserted at the top of the notice, replacing the merge field. Scroll through the notices—you should have a total of seven individually addressed notices. A page break at the bottom of the notice main document ensures that each merged notice prints on a separate page.

Figure 7.16
The completed notices all individually addressed.

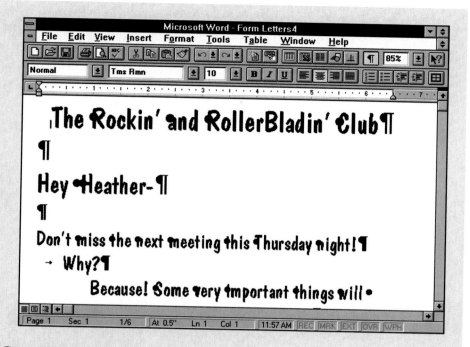

⑫ Click the Print icon on the toolbar.

Clicking the Print icon sends the notices to the printer.

⑬ Double-click the Control-menu box.

Double-clicking the Control-menu box closes the document window. Word prompts you to save your changes.

⑭ Choose No.

In most cases, you don't need to save the results of a merge because you can always merge the two files together again. Now, save the changes to CLUBLIST.DOC and CLUBENV.DOC; then close all open documents.

If you have completed your session on the computer, exit Word for Windows and the Windows Program Manager before turning off the computer. Otherwise, continue with the "Applying Your Skills" case studies at the end of this project.

Checking Your Skills

True/False

For each of the following statements, check *T* or *F* to indicate whether the statement is true or false.

__T __F **1.** Merge fields in both the main document(s) and the data source must match exactly.

__T __F **2.** The main document contains the information you insert into the data source.

__T __F **3.** The Data Form dialog box lets you enter the merge fields you want to use in the data source.

__T __F **4.** Each piece of information in the data source is called a record.

__T __F **5.** You can create a main document from scratch or from an existing document.

Multiple Choice

Circle the letter of the correct answer for each of the following.

1. The _____ contains the information you want to insert when you merge the files.

    a. main document

    b. data source

    c. file manager

    d. data file

2. A(n) _____ is the combination of a data source and a main document.

    a. association

    b. file connection

    c. merge

    d. file relationship

3. When you insert a merge field into a main document, it looks like _____.

    a. F {FirstName}

    b. MergeField {FirstName}

    c. FIELD (FirstName)

    d. <<FirstName>>

   4. You can create an envelope main document from the _____ dialog box.

      a. Data Form

      b. Merge

      c. Mail Merge Helper

      d. Create Data Source

   5. You must define the _____ before you can enter information in the data source.

      a. field codes

      b. merge fields

      c. data fields

      d. merge codes

Completion

In the blank provided, write the correct answer for each of the following statements.

   1. When you merge a data source with a main document, a new document is created for every _____ in the data source.

   2. The _____ file contains merge fields where the information from the data source is inserted.

   3. You can create both data source and main documents from the _____ dialog box.

   4. You can have as many _____ in a record as you need.

   5. You can merge different _____ files with the same data source in a merge.

Applying Your Skills

Take a few minutes to practice the skills you have learned in this project by completing the "On Your Own" and "Brief Cases" case studies.

On Your Own

Creating a Mail Merge with Your Resume Cover Letter

Create a short data source with the names and addresses of prospective employers. Then open the cover letter, and modify it by adding merge fields where the names and addresses should appear. You also create envelopes with the merge fields for the names and addresses. Once you finish these tasks, you merge the files together to produce personalized cover letters and envelopes.

To Set Up the Cover Letter Merge

1. Open the PROJ0702.DOC; then save it as **CVRLTR2.DOC**, and identify CVRLTR2.DOC as the main document.

2. Create a data source with the following names and addresses. When you create the data source, make sure you include the company name field. Also, add a new field for a salutation (Mr. College, for example) for each individual.

Mr. Chris College	**Ms. Mary Spangler**
Seatek Enterprises	**Taylor Homes**
100 Elm Street	**100 West 5th**
Indianapolis, IN 46032	**Carmel, IN 46290**
Ms. Lynn Stewart	**Mr. Bill Jelson**
Emily Sayer Interprises	**Advanced Data Systems**
8701 North IH-43	**Cross Park Business Park**
Bldg. 6, Suite 11	**1100 Jackson Blvd.**
Indianapolis, IN 46032	**Indianapolis, IN 46290**

3. Save the data source as **LETRLST.DOC**.

4. Switch to the CVRLTR2.DOC file, and replace the name and address with merge fields for the names, addresses, and salutation in the data source.

5. Create an envelope main document with fields for the name and addresses. Save it as **CVRENV.DOC**.

6. Merge the cover letter and envelope main documents with the data source.

7. Print both the merged letters and the merged envelopes.

Brief Cases

Creating a Mail Merge for the Radio Ad Copy

Use the skills you have learned in this project to set up and execute a merge that will produce a cover letter to accompany the ad copy you created in Project 2.

To Create the Cover Letter

1. Define a data source with merge fields for name, company, and address information. You should probably include a formal salutation.

2. Type in several names and addresses for local radio stations (KLBJ, KEYI, and KBTO).

3. Save the data source as **RADIODAT.DOC**.

4. Create a short cover letter main document with merge fields for the name and address information.

5. Insert a page break at the end of the letter so the merged letters print out on separate pages.

6. Save the cover letter main document as **RADIOLTR.DOC**.

7. Create an envelope main document.

8. Save the envelope main document as **RADIOENV.DOC**.

9. Merge the cover letter and envelope main documents with the data source.

10. Print both the merged cover letter and merged envelopes.

Project 8

Using Macros and Templates

Automating Your Work

In this project, you learn how to

➤ Record a Macro

➤ Run a Macro

➤ Add a Sample Macro Template

➤ Run a Sample Macro

➤ Use Word Templates

Why Would I Do This?

Now that you have seen a variety of the tasks that you can perform in Word, you may want to know how you can make accomplishing these tasks faster and easier. Although some word processing tasks only require a step or two, others require a series of steps, which means you spend a lot of time making selections in menus and dialog boxes. Word gives you a tool to speed up these tasks—a macro.

Macros are small computer programs that you can write in Word to speed up repetitive tasks. Using your own name and address information and the instructions provided in this project, you learn how to record a macro that types your return address for you. You then play (or run) the macro in a sample document. Finally, you run a font sample generator macro that comes with the Word 6.0 program.

Word provides another feature to help you automate your work—templates. A *template* is a document with built-in formatting—all you have to do is fill in the information. Word includes a large selection of professionally designed template documents for your use. In this project, you use a fax cover sheet template to create a cover sheet.

Macro
A series of actions that can be defined, recorded, and used again later.

Template
A document that contains boiler-plate text and formatting.

Lesson 1: Recording a Macro

Creating a macro in Word is like making a tape recording. When you record a song with a tape recorder, you insert a tape, press Record, and record the song as it plays on the radio. When you want to listen to the song again, you insert the tape, press Play, and listen as the song plays from the tape.

When you create a macro in Word, you record your actions (keystrokes and commands). For example, you can record a macro to type your company name, to insert page numbers, or to set up the format for a formal report. *Running* a macro is simply playing back the actions you recorded. Virtually anything you can do in Word can be done using a macro. Try recording a simple macro now.

Run
To execute or "play" a macro.

To Record a Macro

❶ Using a new document, choose Tools, Macro.

The Macro dialog box appears as shown in Figure 8.1.

continues

To Record a Macro (continued)

Figure 8.1
The Macro dialog box.

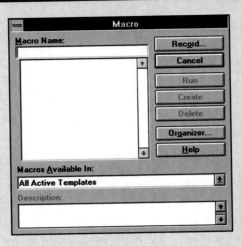

❷ **Choose Record.**

The Record Macro dialog box appears (see Figure 8.2). You need to assign a name for your macro now. A macro name can have up to 80 characters (but no spaces), and you can use upper- and lower-case letters if you choose (for example, InsertPgNum).

Figure 8.2
The Record Macro
dialog box.

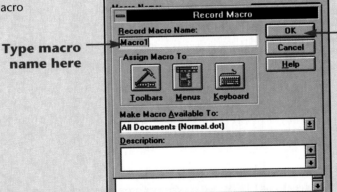

Type macro
name here

Click here to
record macro

❸ **Type ReturnAddress; then choose OK.**

The macro is assigned the name ReturnAddress. The Record Macro dialog box then closes, and you are returned to the document window (see Figure 8.3). A small Macro Record toolbar with two buttons displays on-screen, and the REC indicator on the status bar becomes boldface. The mouse pointer displays with a tiny cassette tape icon attached to it.

❹ **Type your name and your address.**

You should type your name and address as you want them to appear when you play the macro in a letter or envelope document. Traditionally, your name and street address appear on separate lines; your city, state, and zip code information appear on the same line. See Figure 8.3 for a sample return address.

Figure 8.3
A sample return address.

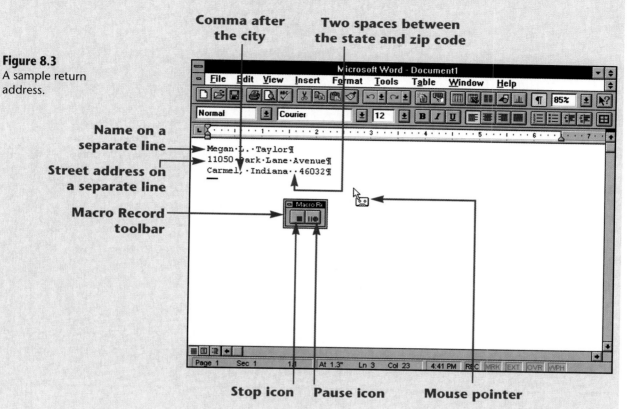

Comma after the city

Two spaces between the state and zip code

Name on a separate line

Street address on a separate line

Macro Record toolbar

Stop icon   **Pause icon**   **Mouse pointer**

If you have problems...

If you make a mistake, don't worry about it—just backspace over the mistake and type the correct information. The macro plays so quickly that you probably won't see any of these extra steps.

When you record a macro, don't include unnecessary cursor movements. For example, if you press Ctrl+Home before you type your return address while recording the macro, the macro performs that keystroke when it runs. The insertion point moves to the top of the document and the return address will be inserted there (instead of at the bottom of the document). If you have included unwanted cursor movement actions in the macro, stop recording the macro (see the following steps), and start over.

continues

To Record a Macro (continued)

When you finish the macro keystrokes, you need to turn off the macro recorder. If you forget to turn the recorder off, Word continues to record keystrokes until you exit the program or turn the recorder off.

5 **Choose Tools; then choose Macro.**

Notice that the Record button has changed to the Stop Recording button.

6 **Choose Stop Recording.**

The macro recorder has been turned off. When you turn the recorder off, Word saves the macro with the macro name you chose earlier.

7 **Choose Close.**

Choosing Close clears the Macro dialog box. The Macro Record toolbar disappears from the screen, and the regular mouse pointer displays in the document window.

8 **Press ⏎Enter three or four times.**

This action inserts blank lines underneath your name. This way, when you run the macro, you can tell the difference between the name you entered and the name the macro typed in for you. Leave this document open for the next lesson.

You can click the buttons on the Macro Record toolbar rather than select from the menus. For example, you can click the Stop icon (see Figure 8.3) to stop recording a macro.

Learn to record macros any time you are performing a repetitive task in a document. It's easy to record a macro as you are performing a task, such as adding a date to a letter. Just use the steps described in this lesson. The keystrokes you enter then serve two purposes—entering text into a document and recording a macro you can use over again later.

What Is a Computer Program?

A computer program is simply a list of commands that tells the computer how to perform a task. The commands tell it where to take the input from, how to process it, and what kind of output goes where.

In essence, by recording a simple macro (as you do in this project), you act as a computer programmer. The actions you record in your macro become the steps of a short and simple computer program.

Some computers, like the one in a digital watch, have all of their programs built-in. You can't change the program to make the watch do anything but tell time. The only commands that you can give the watch are the few that the built-in program was designed to understand.

```
NIGHT-TIME:
    Sleep until you wake up.

WAKING UP:

    If the alarm clock isn't ringing yet,
        leap ahead to NIGHT-TIME routine.
    If it's SATURDAY or SUNDAY,
        leap back to WEEKEND routine.
    Turn off alarm clock.
    Eat breakfast.
    Go to work.
    Work.
    Come home from work.
    Eat dinner.
    Watch sitcoms.
    Leap back to a NIGHT-TIME routine.
WEEKEND:
    Eat breakfast.
    Go for a bike ride.
    Eat lunch.
    Watch sports.
    Eat dinner.
    Watch more sports.
    Leap back to NIGHT-TIME routine
```

Personal computers, however, are designed to let you put in different programs. Just like a VCR can act as a movie theater, an aerobics instructor, or an album of photos of your grandchild (depending on what tape you play), a computer can perform many different tasks depending on the programs you install in the computer. When you use a word processing program, the computer becomes a word processor. When you use a game program, it becomes an arcade.

A computer program can be very complex, often involving hundreds of thousands of individual commands. Because a computer only understands a limited (but useful) set of commands, difficult procedures have to be broken into long strings of these small steps.

People who create computer programs (programmers) rarely do so in the language that the computer directly understands (machine language). Machine language commands are nothing but numbers. Instead, programmers write in languages designed for programming, which allows the programmers to work in a language that is more understandable to them.

These programs are then translated by another program into a form that the computer can directly handle. These translation programs, called compilers, assemblers, and interpreters, break the big steps of the programming language into the smaller, numeric steps that the computer understands.

Compilers and assemblers translate the program into machine language and save the machine language version on disk. An interpreter handles each of the programmer's commands one at a time, translating each command into the smaller commands the machine understands, and then immediately acting on those commands. Because the interpreter tries to translate the program as well as act on the commands every time the program is used, this process is slower than using a program that has been translated ahead of time by a compiler or an assembler.

*For further information relating to this topic, see Unit 3A, "Software,"of **Computers in Your Future** by Marilyn Meyer and Roberta Baber.*

Lesson 2: Running a Macro

Now that you have recorded your macro, you can run (or play) the macro in a document to see it automatically perform the recorded task. The Word installation program installs a NORMAL.DOT file, a template that contains the default settings for all new documents. Word stores any macros that you create in this template so that you have the macros available to use in any document you choose.

Try running the return address macro now.

To Run a Macro

❶ In the document in which you typed your name, choose Tools, Macro from the menu bar.

The Macro dialog box appears. You can select the macro file in the list, or you can type the name in the **M**acro Name text box.

❷ Click the ReturnAddress macro in the Macro Name list box.

The Macro Name list box contains a list of available macros.

❸ Choose Run.

The macro you recorded runs, entering your return address in the document window. Macros enter repetitive information quickly and accurately. Once you record the macro correctly, it stays correct every time you run it.

Before you go on to the next lesson, close the document without saving your changes—this was only a practice macro.

 You can choose to assign macros to a specific template, rather than to the Normal template, which is available to all documents. For example, you might decide to create a Proposal template that contains only those macros that help you generate your proposals.

Lesson 3: Adding a Sample Macro Template

Word includes over 35 sample macros that you can use right away to help you perform repetitive tasks. These samples also provide examples you can study if you start writing your own macros.

The macros that come with Word are stored in the following files: MACRO60.DOT, TABLES.DOT, LAYOUT.DOT, CONVERT.DOT and PRESENT.DOT.

Before you can use these macros, you must make them available for use in other documents by adding them to the Global Templates and Add-ins list box. Try adding a sample macro template now.

To Add a Sample Macro Template

❶ Choose File, Templates.

The Templates and Add-ins dialog box appears, as shown in Figure 8.4.

Figure 8.4
Use the Templates and Add-ins dialog box to add templates to the global template.

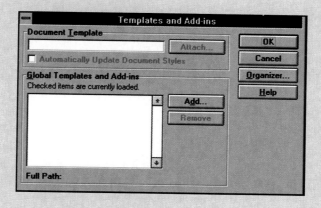

❷ Choose Add.

The Add Template dialog box appears (see Figure 8.5). The Template subdirectory is the current directory in this dialog box. The macro templates, however, are stored in the Macros directory, so you need to change to that directory.

Figure 8.5
Use the Add Template dialog box to add templates to the global template.

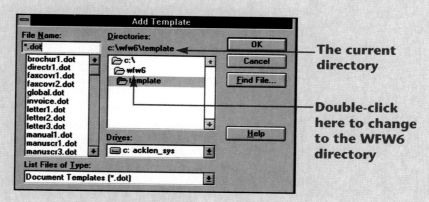

❸ Double-click the WFW6 directory icon.

Double-clicking the WFW6 directory icon changes the directory to the WFW6 directory, allowing you to see all the subdirectories under the WFW6 directory.

❹ Double-click the MACROS directory icon.

Double-clicking the MACROS directory icon opens the Macros subdirectory and displays the template files in the File **N**ame list box (see Figure 8.6).

continues

To Add a Sample Macro Template (continued)

Figure 8.6
The macro template files are shown in the File **N**ame list box.

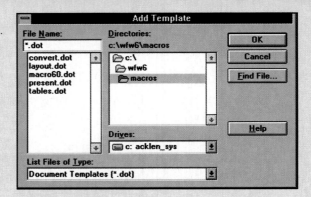

⑤ Click the MACRO60.DOT file, and choose OK.

The MACRO60.DOT template file now appears in the **G**lobal Templates and Add-ins list box (see Figure 8.7). The check box next to the template lets you select and deselect the file once it appears in the list box. When you select the template file, the macro files show up in the Macro dialog box; when you deselect the template file, the macro files do not show up in the Macro dialog box.

Figure 8.7
The Macro template file added to the global template.

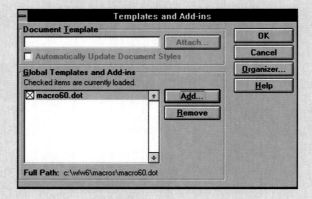

⑥ Choose OK.

Choosing OK closes the Templates and Add-ins dialog box. If you haven't done so already, close the current document before you run the sample macros in Lesson 4.

Lesson 4: Running a Sample Macro

In this lesson, you run a macro from the MACRO60.DOT template file. The macro, FontSampleGenerator, creates a document with a sample of each font available on your system. Try running this sample macro now.

❶ Click the New icon.

Clicking the New icon on the toolbar opens a new document so that you can run the macro.

❷ From the menu bar, choose Tools, Macro.

The Macro dialog box appears with a list of the macros in the MACRO60.DOT template listed in the Macro Name list box (see Figure 8.8).

Figure 8.8
The macros from the MACRO60.DOT template are displayed in the Macro dialog box.

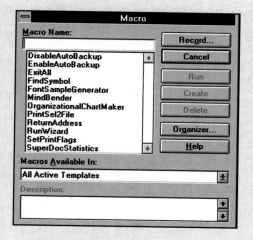

❸ Click the FontSampleGenerator file.

Clicking the file selects the FontSampleGenerator file.

❹ Choose Run.

Choosing **R**un opens the Font Sample Generator dialog box (see Figure 8.9). A message in the lower right corner of the dialog box lets you know how many fonts were found on your system.

Figure 8.9
The Font Sample Generator dialog box.

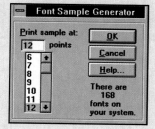

❺ Choose OK.

Choosing OK runs the macro and uses the default of 12 points for the font samples. While the macro runs, the Font Sample Generator dialog box shows the progress. The messages give you the name of

continues

To Run a Sample Macro (continued)

the font as the sample is created, the point size for the sample, and the current font/total fonts counter. A message appears at the bottom of the dialog box stating that you can press ⎡Esc⎤ to cancel the macro.

When the macro finishes, the font sample document opens in the document window (see Figure 8.10). The font samples appear in a two column table. Scroll down through the document to see the variety of font styles on your system.

Figure 8.10
The sample font document created by the FontSampleGenerator macro.

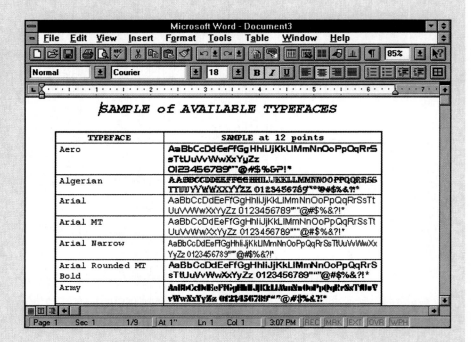

6 Save the document as FONTSAMP.DOC, and close it.

Remember, you can always run the macro again. Whatever you decide, close the document before you continue on to the next lesson.

You can read through a list of sample macros (or print the list if you prefer) by searching for the key word "macros" to locate the Help topic called Recording and Running Macros. At the bottom of this Help screen is a topic called Using the Macros Supplied with Word. Click this Help topic to jump to another Help screen, where you see a Help topic called Supplied Macros. You then click this topic to switch to a Help screen that lists the template files containing the sample macros. Click a template file to get a list of the macros in that template. If you want to print the list, choose **P**rint Topic from the **H**elp **F**ile menu.

Lesson 5: Using Word Templates

Now that you have seen some of the most commonly used formatting commands, you have an appreciation of the effort it takes to create a properly formatted and professional-looking document. By using the predefined document templates Word offers, you can eliminate much of the time and effort in creating common types of documents. These templates are predefined documents with all the formatting built in—you just fill in the blanks and print.

Word includes a wide variety of templates, from desktop publishing documents to calendars to legal briefs. One of the most frequently used form documents is a fax cover sheet. Try filling out the form template for a fax cover sheet now.

To Use a Word Template

❶ In a blank document window, choose File, New.

The New dialog box opens, which lets you select a template to use for the new document (see Figure 8.11).

Figure 8.11
The New dialog box with a list of available templates.

❷ Choose Faxcovr2 in the Template list box.

The Faxcovr2 cover sheet provides a contemporary design for you to use.

❸ Choose OK.

Choosing OK opens the Faxcovr2 template in a new document window (see Figure 8.12). Word automatically fills in the current date and time. The rest of the markers remind you what information you need to type. To fill in the fax cover sheet, you delete the text (and the brackets), and then enter your information.

continues

To Use a Word Template (continued)

Figure 8.12
The Faxcovr2 template open in a document window.

Select and delete the markers

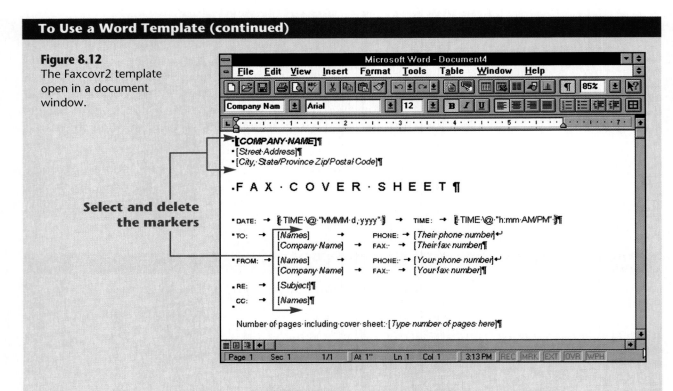

❹ **Select the [Company Name] marker, and press** Del.

The fastest way to select the marker is to click in the selection area (inside the left margin). Pressing Del removes the selected text.

❺ **Type ISU Rollerblading Club.**

The built-in style for the company name uses all capital letters for emphasis.

❻ **Select and delete the [Street Address] marker; then type 1963 Hazelton Street.**

This is the street address for the Rollerblading Club.

❼ **Select and delete the [City, State/Province Zip/Postal Code] marker, and type Indianapolis, Indiana 46033.**

This action completes the company and address information of the sender.

❽ Select and delete the rest of the markers, and enter the following information:

Beth Huxtuble	317-555-3801
Huxtuble Agency	317-555-3737
Megan L. Taylor	317-555-1160
ISU Rollerblading Club	317-555-0888

Ad copy in the student newspaper

Rebecca Smith-Bailey, Benjamin Taylor

3

Please look over the enclosed ad copy and call me at your convenience so we might discuss the changes. Thanks!

The completed fax cover sheet should now look like the one shown in Figure 8.13.

Figure 8.13
The fax cover sheet is now ready to send.

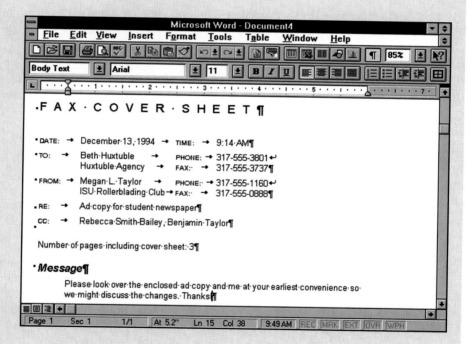

❾ Print the fax cover sheet.

If you think you may send fax documents to this recipient, you should save the completed cover sheet. Otherwise, just close the document without saving the changes. You can always use the template again when necessary.

If you have completed your session on the computer, exit Word for Windows and the Windows Program Manager before turning off the computer. Otherwise, continue with the "Applying Your Skills" case studies at the end of this project.

If you have a fax board in your computer, you can fax directly from Word. When you open the Print dialog box, choose Printer to open the Print Setup dialog box, where you can select the fax board as the current printer. Choose **P**rint—Word then sends the document to the fax. Make sure you switch back to your printer when you are finished; otherwise you will send future documents directly to the fax board. In addition, certain fax programs automatically add a Fax menu command on the **F**ile menu, so you don't have to worry about switching printers.

Checking Your Skills

True/False

For each of the following statements, check *T* or *F* to indicate whether the statement is true or false.

__T __F **1.** Creating a macro is similar to recording a cassette tape in a tape recorder.

__T __F **2.** Macro names can be from one to 122 characters.

__T __F **3.** A macro is like a small program that you can write in Word.

__T __F **4.** The sample macros are stored in templates in the Templates subdirectory.

__T __F **5.** Word uses markers in the document templates to remind you what information you need to enter.

Multiple Choice

Circle the letter of the correct answer for each of the following.

1. Which of the following is not a valid macro file name?

   a. LETTERCLOSE

   b. Header Doc

   c. PrintLetter

   d. InsertPageNumbering

2. The _____ menu contains the **M**acro command.

   a. **E**dit

   b. F**o**rmat

   c. **T**ools

   d. **I**nsert

3. Word stores its sample macro files in _____.

   a. macro files

   b. document templates

   c. the WINDOWS directory

   d. the WFW6 directory

4. Word has _____ different template files that contain sample macros.

    a. seven

    b. three

    c. six

    d. five

5. A document template is used to _____.

    a. ensure that saved information is stored in memory

    b. display buttons on the Word toolbar

    c. format the document on-screen

    d. create commonly used documents with a minimum of formatting

Completion

In the blank provided, write the correct answer for each of the following statements.

1. Word includes over _____ sample macros that you can use right away.

2. If you need to perform actions you don't want recorded in a macro, click the _____ button.

3. A macro records your _____ so that you can play them back later.

4. The FontSampleGenerator macro creates a document with a sample of every _____ available in Word.

5. Document _____ are documents with the formatting already built-in.

Applying Your Skills

Take a few minutes to practice the skills you have learned in this project by completing the "On Your Own" and "Brief Cases" case studies.

On Your Own

Creating a Routing Slip Macro

This time, record a macro that creates a routing slip with the names of the members of the Rollerblading Club. Because you are the club's secretary, you have to distribute newsletters and flyers to the members. The routing slip will consist of a 5-character underscore line followed by a tab, then each member's name. When the member has read the information, they fill in their initials and pass it on to the next member.

To Create the Routing Slip Macro

1. Name a macro called **routslip**.

2. Once you turn the recorder on, type the following information:

    _____**Heather West**

    _____**Jay Stephens**

    _____**Kelly Jelson**

    _____**Jon Crain**

    _____**Jimmy Gardner**

    _____**Sharon Orsborn**

    _____**Chuck Anderson**

3. Turn off the macro recorder.

4. Play the macro.

Brief Cases

Use the skills you have learned in Project 8 to create two macros for Sound Byte Music. The first macro is a memo form from you (the owner) to the employees. The macro types out the memo title and headings. You can enter the subject, date, and memo text later. The second macro is a fax cover sheet from Sound Byte Music to a large radio station (KBIG) that you frequently send faxes to.

To Create the Memo Macro

1. Name a macro called **MemoForm**.

2. Type the following information:

    Sound Byte Music Memo

    TO: **Very Cool Sound Byte Music Employees**

    FROM: **The Boss**

    DATE:

    SUBJECT:

3. Turn off the macro recorder.

To Create the Fax Macro

1. Name a macro called **KBIGFaxCoverSheet**.

2. Use the Faxcovr2 template to create the fax cover sheet.

3. Type the following information in the fax cover sheet template:

> **Sound Byte Music**
> **13 Jackson Drive**
> **Indianapolis, IN 46232**
>
> **Jamie Stewart**
> **(513) 555-5244**
> **KBIG**
> **(513) 555-5251**
> **Kevin James**
> **(513) 555-1160**
> **Sound Byte Music**
> **(513) 555-1360**
> **New Release from River City Records**
> **Leave blank**
> **Leave blank**
>
> **Leave the message area blank**

4. Turn off the macro recorder.

5. Fill in the rest of the blanks, as necessary.

6. Print the fax cover sheet.

Appendix A

Working with Windows

In this appendix, you learn how to

- ➤ Start Windows
- ➤ Use the Mouse in Windows
- ➤ Understand the Windows Desktop
- ➤ Understand the Program Manager
- ➤ Exit Windows

Why Would I Do This?

Graphical user interface
An easy-to-use method of combining graphics, menus, and plain English commands so that the user communicates with the computer.

Microsoft Windows is a powerful operating environment that enables you to access the power of DOS without memorizing DOS commands and syntax. Windows uses a *graphical user interface* (GUI) so that you can easily see on-screen the tools you need to complete specific file and program management tasks.

This appendix, an overview of the Windows environment, is designed to help you learn the basics of Windows.

Lesson 1: Starting Windows

Many computers are set to open in Windows. If your computer does not automatically open in Windows, however, you can easily access the program.

Starting Windows

To start Windows from the DOS command prompt, follow these steps:

Window
A rectangular area on-screen in which you view program icons, applications, or documents.

1. Type **WIN**.

2. Press ⏎Enter. Windows begins loading. When it is loaded, you see the Program Manager window open on-screen.

Icon
A picture that represents a group window, an application, a document, or other element in a GUI-based program.

The Program Manager *window* includes many different elements, such as the menu bar, title bar, and *icons*. (You open windows, start applications, and select items by selecting the appropriate icon.) Your Program Manager window may look different from the window used in this book's illustrations. For example, you may have different program group icons across the bottom of the Program Manager window (see Figure A.1).

Figure A.1
The first time you start Windows, a group window may be open on the desktop.

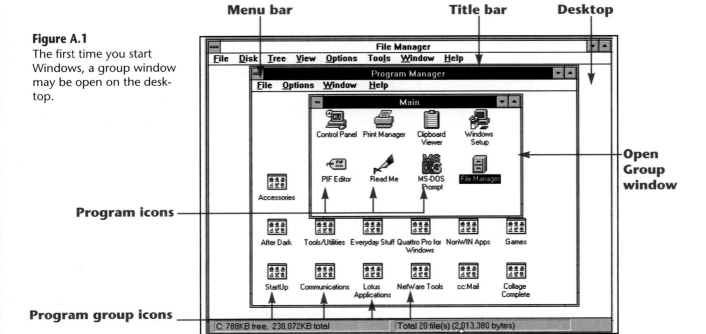

Program icons

Program group icons

Lesson 2: Using the Mouse in Windows

Mouse

A pointing device used in many programs to make choices, select data, and otherwise communicate with the computer.

Windows is designed for use with a *mouse*. Although you can get by with just a keyboard, using a mouse is much easier. This book assumes that you are using a mouse.

In the Windows desktop, you can use a mouse to

➤ Open windows

➤ Close windows

➤ Open menus

➤ Choose menu commands

➤ Rearrange on-screen items, such as icons and windows

Mouse pointer

A symbol that appears on-screen to indicate the current location of the mouse.

The position of the mouse is indicated on-screen by a *mouse pointer*. Usually, the mouse pointer is an arrow, but it sometimes changes shape depending on the current action.

Mouse pad

A pad that provides a uniform surface for a mouse to slide on.

On-screen the mouse pointer moves according to the movements of the mouse on your desk or on a *mouse pad*. To move the mouse pointer, simply move the mouse.

There are three basic mouse actions:

➤ *Click*. To point to an item, and then press and quickly release the left mouse button. You click to select an item, such as an option on a menu. To cancel a selection, click an empty area of the desktop. Unless otherwise specified, you use the left mouse button for all mouse actions.

➤ *Double-click*. To point to an item, and then press and release the left mouse button twice, as quickly as possible. You double-click to open or close windows and to start applications from icons.

➤ *Drag*. To point to an item, and then press and hold down the left mouse button as you move the pointer to another location, and then release the mouse button. You drag to resize windows, move icons, and scroll.

> **If you have problems...**
>
> If you try to double-click but nothing happens, you may not be clicking fast enough. Try again.

Lesson 3: Understanding the Windows Desktop

Desktop

The background of the Windows screen, on which windows, icons, and dialog boxes appear.

Your screen provides a *desktop*, the background for Windows. On the desktop, each application is displayed in its own window (hence the name Windows). All windows have the same set of elements that enable you to move, resize, and manipulate the window.

If you have multiple windows open, they may overlap on the desktop, just as papers on your desk can be stacked one on top of the other. You may have one or more windows open when you start Windows.

The Title Bar

Across the top of each window is its title bar. At the right side of the title bar is the minimize button for reducing windows to icons and the maximize button for expanding windows to fill the desktop. At the left side of the title bar is the Control-menu box, a box with a small hyphen in it. The Control-menu box activates a window's Control menu.

Menus

Menus enable you to select options to perform functions or carry out commands (see Figure A.2). The Control menu, for example, enables you to control the size and position of its window.

Figure A.2
Every open window has a title bar, used to identify the contents of the window. Menus, like the Control menu shown here, enable you to choose commands without remembering DOS syntax, switches, or parameters.

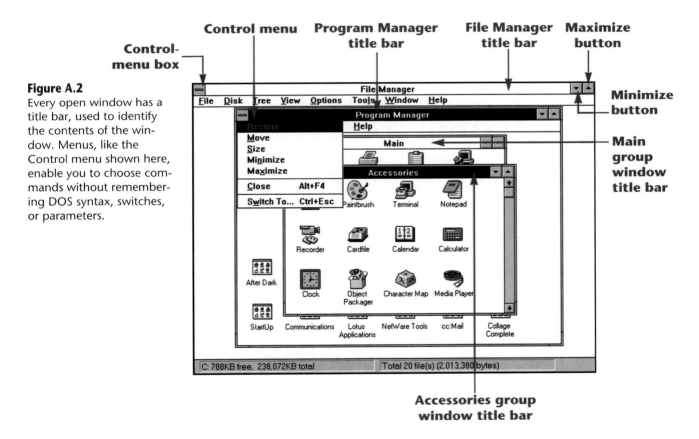

Accessories group window title bar

Dialog box
A window that opens on-screen to provide information about the current action or to ask the user to enter additional information to complete the action.

Dialog Boxes

Some menu options require you to enter additional information. When you select one of these options, a *dialog box* opens (see Figure A.3). You either type the additional information into a text box, select from a list of options, or select a button.

Buttons

Buttons are on-screen areas with which you can select actions or commands. Most dialog boxes have at least a Cancel button, which stops the current activity and returns to the preceding screen; an OK button, which accepts the current activity; and a Help button, which opens a Help window (see Figure A.3).

Figure A.3
In a dialog box, you provide additional information to complete the command. The Search dialog box of the Help feature has buttons you click to set options or choose commands.

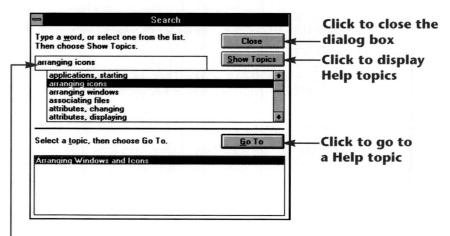

Click to close the dialog box

Click to display Help topics

Click to go to a Help topic

Enter additional information here

Lesson 4: Understanding the Program Manager

The Program Manager is the central Microsoft Windows program. When you start Microsoft Windows, the Program Manager starts automatically. When you exit Microsoft Windows, you exit the Program Manager. You can't run Microsoft Windows if you are not running the Program Manager.

Program groups
Application programs organized into a set that can be accessed through a program group window.

The Program Manager does what its name implies—it manages programs. You use the Program Manager to organize programs into groups called *program groups*. Usually, programs in a group are related, either by function (such as a group of accessories) or by usage (such as a group of programs used to compile a monthly newsletter).

Each program group is represented by a program group icon. In each program group window, you see the icons for each program item in the group (see Figure A.4).

To be comfortable using Windows, you need to know how to control your Windows desktop, which in large part means controlling the windows themselves.

You can open, close, resize, and reposition all the windows that appear in Windows, including the Program Manager.

Opening a Window

To open a window, double-click the appropriate icon (see Figure A.4). When you double-click a program group icon, you open a group window. When you double-click a program icon, you start that program.

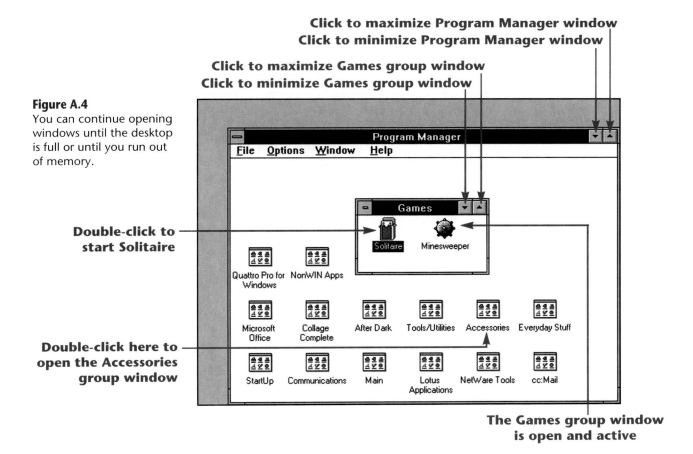

Click to maximize Program Manager window
Click to minimize Program Manager window

Click to maximize Games group window
Click to minimize Games group window

Figure A.4
You can continue opening windows until the desktop is full or until you run out of memory.

Double-click to start Solitaire

Double-click here to open the Accessories group window

The Games group window is open and active

If you have problems...

If a Control menu opens instead of a window, you are not double-clicking fast enough. Try again, or choose **R**estore from the Control menu.

Don't worry if your screen looks different from the screens used to illustrate this book. Your desktop may be organized differently. You still can perform all the same tasks. You can also use the Control menu to open a window. Click the icon once to display the Control menu. Then click **R**estore.

Maximizing a Window

Maximize
To increase the size of a window until it covers the desktop.

You can *maximize* a window to fill the entire desktop. Maximizing a window gives you more space in which to work.

To maximize a window, do one of the following:

➤ Click the maximize button at the far right of the window's title bar. This button has an arrowhead pointing up.

➤ Choose Ma**x**imize from the window's Control menu (refer to Figure A.4).

Minimizing a Window

Minimize
To reduce a window to an icon.

You can *minimize* a window that you are not currently using.

To minimize a window, take one of the following actions:

➤ Click the minimize button on the title bar. This button has an arrowhead pointing down (refer to Figure A.4).

➤ Choose Minimize from the window's Control menu.

Program group windows, such as the Main group, are reduced to program group icons at the bottom of the Program Manager. Application, utility, or document icons are positioned at the bottom of the desktop, behind any active windows. The application that has been minimized is still active; it is just out of the way.

Arranging the Windows on Your Desktop

Tile
To arrange open windows on the desktop so that they do not overlap.

Sometimes a desktop becomes so cluttered with open windows that you cannot tell what you are using. When that happens, you can choose either to *tile* or to *cascade* the open windows on-screen so that you can see them all.

To arrange the windows on the desktop, follow these steps:

Cascade
To arrange open windows on the desktop so that they overlap, but at least a portion of each window is displayed.

1. Choose **W**indow from the menu bar to display the Window menu.

2. Choose one of the following:

➤ **T**ile, to arrange the windows on-screen so that none are overlapping (see Figure A.5).

➤ **C**ascade, to arrange the windows on-screen so that they overlap (see Figure A.6).

Figure A.5
The windows are tiled on the desktop.

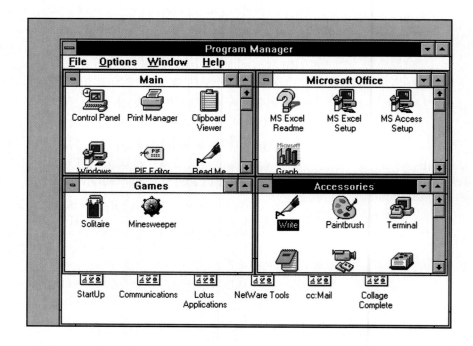

Figure A.6
The windows are cascaded on the desktop.

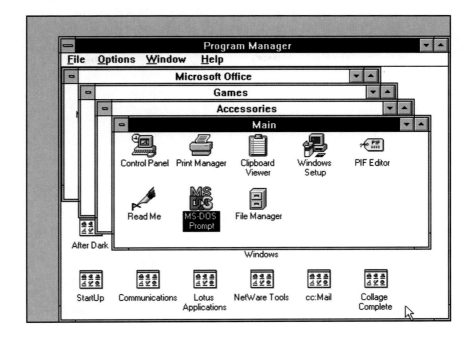

Closing a Window

To close a window, take one of the following actions:

➤ Choose **C**lose from the window's Control menu.

➤ Choose **C**lose from the window's **F**ile menu.

➤ Double-click the Control menu button. (To open the Control menu, click the Control menu button at the far left end of the window's title bar.)

If you have problems...

If the Exit Windows dialog box appears, you probably clicked the Control-menu button for the Program Manager rather than the Control-menu button for the window you want to close. Click Cancel.

Lesson 5: Exiting Windows

You should always exit Windows before turning off your computer.

To exit Windows:

1. Close all open windows and applications.

2. Point to **F**ile in the menu bar, and click the left mouse button.

3. Point to E**x**it Windows, and click the left mouse button. Windows prompts you to confirm that you want to exit.

4. Move the mouse pointer to OK, and click the left mouse button. Windows closes, and the DOS command prompt is displayed.

As a shortcut, simply double-click the Control-menu box at the far left of the Program Manager title bar. Windows asks you to confirm that you want to exit. Choose OK.

INDEX